SERMONS FROM THE PSALMS

BOOKS BY THE SAME AUTHOR

SERMONS FROM THE PSALMS

By

CLOVIS G. CHAPPELL

ABINGDON PRESS

NEW YORK   ●   NASHVILLE

SERMONS FROM THE PSALMS

Copyright MCMXXXI by Lamar & Whitmore

SET UP, PRINTED, AND BOUND BY THE
PARTHENON PRESS, AT NASHVILLE,
TENNESSEE, UNITED STATES OF AMERICA

THIS BOOK IS DEDICATED
TO MY AUNTS

MRS. CARRIE RUSSELL AND MISS LUCK HART

WHO HAVE FOUND MUCH SUNSHINE
ALONG A ROAD THAT HAS
HAD ITS SHADOWS

CONTENTS

7

8 SERMONS FROM THE PSALMS

CAPITALIZING OUR CALAMITIES

Psalm 119: 71 (Moffatt)

"It is good for me to have been in trouble."

HERE is a man looking back upon his yesterdays. He is taking a glance at the way along which he has come. That way has not been altogether through green pastures and beside still waters. Sometimes it has dipped down into dreary canyons or climbed up over toilsome mountains. His has not been a sheltered life. More than one tempest has broken upon him. Often have rude winds pounded him with their cruel fists. Here and there treasures to which he clung with passionate devotion have been ruthlessly snatched from his hands. More than once has his face been wet by a gush of hot and blinding tears.

But as he looks back upon those days of stress and strain he is conscious of the fact that they have not resulted half so disastrously as he thought they would when he was passing through them. In fact, he sees now, with joyous amazement, that they have brought him no abiding harm at all. On the contrary, they have brought abiding good. The very trouble that he thought was going to work his utter undoing has been the making of him. His losses have become gains,

9

and his calamities have been changed into capital. "It is good for me to have been in trouble," he cries in humble gladness. And looking back to those ugly yesterdays through eyes washed bright by tears, they somehow lose their ugliness. "As the mountains hard by look jagged and scarred, but in the distance repose in their soft, mellow robes of purple and haze, so the rough present fades into the past, tender, sweet, and beautiful."

I

Now we are separated from this ancient psalmist by seas and centuries and continents. We are separated from him by widely differing customs and widely differing modes of living. Yet we are like him in this, that we have our troubles. We, too, have been through some trying conflicts out of which some of us have come sorely wounded. There have been times when rude winds have blown upon us that have dashed our houses of happiness to pieces. At times our eyes, even as his, have been blinded by tears. Few of us get very far into life without realizing that there is something more than blind pessimism in those words of Job: "Man is born unto trouble, as the sparks fly upward." Therefore we are interested in the struggles and trials of this psalmist because he is so like ourselves.

Just the nature of this man's trouble we are not told. His may have been some obvious and visible calamity that every one could see. For weary years his own life may have been one long battle with pain. Or, as in the case of Ezekiel, God may have taken away the light of his eyes at a stroke. Or he may have suffered from some sorrow of which the world did not know. He may have bled from a hidden wound. He may have worn sackcloth within upon his flesh while he showed to the world only the royal purple of a cheerful countenance. He may have wept in secret over some sordid tragedy of his own or of one dear to him, that was all the harder to bear because he dared not share it with even his dearest friend.

But though we do not know the nature of his trouble, we are sure of this, that his life had not been without its tragic experiences. Neither have yours and mine. Life has not been all shadow with any of us, thank God! But neither has it been all sunshine. We have seen our skies suddenly grow dark. We have felt the bleak chill of dear dreams that never came true. And, even to those to whom this experience has not yet come, the chances are overwhelmingly great that one day it will be. I know that to some these words sound very like the croakings of a pessimist. But it is not unkind to say that one day, soon or late, even to you will come the testing of trouble. We may sail for many days upon smooth seas. Then suddenly the tempest is upon us. We realize that even to us the seemingly impossible has happened. With some life deals far more roughly than with others. But to all, soon or late, there come gray days of bewilderment and trouble.

II

Now, since trouble is so nearly a universal human experience, what are we going to do about it? There are three attitudes that we may assume in the face of life's perplexing calamities.

1. There is the attitude of surrender. There are those who give over the fight at the very first painful wound that they receive in the battle. There are those who walk along cheerfully till by and by some cruel fate trips them and they fall flat. Having fallen, instead of rising to their feet to renew the struggle, they lie and whine and bewail their hard lot. They spend the remainder of their days in a kind of spiritual invalidism. They declare that life has never dealt so harshly with any others as with themselves. They focus all their attention upon their own wretchedness. Thus surrendering they add both to their own troubles and to those of their fellows.

When I first went away to school I boarded in a home where there were three lovely children, two boys and a girl. But the destroying hand of disease was laid upon the girl and she faded like a flower. Of course, her mother's heart was broken. We were not surprised at that. That was only to be expected. But what was surprising was that this mother seemed to forget her two children that were still left to her. She seemed to forget her husband, who was almost as heartbroken as herself. She had formerly been active in her church, but she forgot all religious and social duties. She denied herself both to her loved ones and to her friends. She shut herself in with her sorrow and let it eat her heart out. Instead of going bravely forward in the fear of God and doing her duty, she gave over the fight and surrendered unconditionally to this first great sorrow of her life.

The same tragic blunder was made by Miss Havisham in *Great Expectations*. She was to be married, you remember. The guests were gathered. The wedding feast was being prepared. The wedding cake was on the table. The bride was decked in her bridal costume. But the bridegroom never came. Therefore her watch and every clock in the house was stopped at twenty minutes to nine, the hour of her humiliation, the hour of her first and one great sorrow. All sunlight was shut out of her home. She lived in the dark except for the light of candles. Her wedding cake stood on the table till the cobwebs wrapped it round and it became the homing place of spiders and mice. Her once white wedding gown hung in yellow decay about her shrunken figure. For her all life had stopped at the hour of her tragic disappointment, twenty minutes to nine. She, too, met her sorrow with unconditional surrender.

What a terrible tragedy is the life of Judas! But what is the climax of that tragedy? It is not altogether in the fact that he betrayed his Lord. It is not the

pangs of hell that got hold upon him in the damning
realization of the terrible crime of which he had been
guilty.   The supreme tragedy of his life was rather
this: That after his deed of treachery he did not dare
to make a new start.   His betrayal was ugly enough,
God knows.   But to have been too cowardly to pick up
the shattered ruins of his broken life and start again,
that was the thing that wrecked him.   More deadly
even than his kiss of treachery was his failure to come
back to the Master whom he had so deeply wronged
and ask for a chance to make another start.   Instead of
doing this he surrendered, took the coward's way that
is all too common to-day, and flung out of life by
suicide.

"Did you tackle the trouble that came your way
    With a resolute heart and cheerful?
Or hide your face from the light of day
    With a craven soul and fearful?
Oh, a trouble's a ton, or a trouble's an ounce,
    Or a trouble is what you make it,
And it isn't the fact that you're hurt that counts,
    But only—how did you take it?

You are beaten to earth? Well, well, what's that!
    Come up with a smiling face.
It's nothing against you to fall down flat,
    But to lie there—that's disgrace.
The harder you're thrown, why, the higher you bounce;
    Be proud of your blackened eye!
It isn't the fact that you're licked that counts;
    It's how did you fight—and why?

And though you be done to the death, what then?
  If you battled the best you could,
If you played your part in the world of men,
  Why, the Critic will call it good.
Death comes with a crawl, or comes with a pounce,
  And whether he's slow or spry,
It isn't the fact that you're dead that counts,
  But only—how did you die?"

2. Then we may allow our troubles to make us hard and cynical. This is only another way of surrender. This is the surrender of the strong, while the other is the surrender of the weak. There are those who gather strength by the buffetings through which they pass. But through their grim fightings they overdevelop their pugnacity. They come to view all weakness with scorn and contempt rather than with sympathy. They say to their weaker brother, "Why do you not fight as I did?" Such become rocklike in their nature. But they are like the rock upon which the ship crashes to go down to its death rather than like the shadow of a great rock in a weary land where tired travelers may find refreshment and rest. There are few sadder losses than a lost sorrow. Such is the sorrow that embitters rather than sweetens and makes tender and sympathetic.

In Hawthorne's "Scarlet Letter" there are three outstanding characters. There is the prodigal wife, Hester Prynne. There is the unfaithful minister, Arthur Dimmesdale, the partner in her sin. There is the wronged husband, Roger Chillingworth. All these sin and all suffer. The sin of the woman is proclaimed to the world by the baby she holds in her arms as she stands on the pedestal of shame. It is further blazoned by the scarlet letter that she is compelled to wear upon her bosom. She suffers, but her suffering is small in comparison with that of the young minister whose sin is unsuspected, save by Roger Chillingworth. But the supreme sufferer, I am sure, is the wronged husband. In seeking revenge he hangs like a terrible bloodhound upon the track of the man who has wrecked his home. He watches him with fiendish glee as he writhes in his agony. At last one night he tortures him to the pedestal of shame and compels him to stand where Hester had stood seven years before. It is terrible to be the victim of a hate like that, but it is far more terrible to be the possessor of such a hate. Roger Chillingworth suffered a great wrong in the loss of his wife, but by far his greatest loss was in that he allowed this wrong to kill his better self and make him unspeakably hard and bitter and cruel.

3. Then there is the group to which this psalmist belongs. These refuse to surrender to their sorrows either by turning cowards or becoming calloused and hard. Instead, they make capital out of their calamities and change their losses into gain. It is of these we can sing:

"Ye spread and span like the catholic man who hath mightily won
  God out of knowledge and good out of infinite pain
  And sight out of blindness and purity out of a stain."

Therefore, it is this group that find life most worth
while.   It is to this group that the world owes its
supreme debt.   They are the most useful and winsome
souls that we know.   Of course, there may be helpful
people who have known little of sorrow; but, as a rule,
by far the most helpful are those who have had their
hearts broken.   They are those who have been to school
in Gethsemane, but whose very want has been changed
into wealth.

III

Now, capitalizing our calamities is one of the finest
of all fine arts.   What knowledge is more to be coveted
than that of changing our pains into palms, our crosses
into crowns?   Years ago certain scientists undertook
to find a method of extracting the gold out of the brine
of the ocean.   What a marvelous discovery that would
have been had they succeeded.   It would have revolu-
tionized commerce.   But there is an infinitely more
priceless secret that we may discover through Jesus
Christ our Lord.   We may learn how to extract the
gold of a larger manhood and of a larger womanhood
out of the brine of human sorrow and human tears.
How can we learn this secret?

1. Let us believe in the possibility of it.   Years ago
a man named Paul desired with burning eagerness to
be allowed to preach the gospel in Rome, then the very
center of the world.   But he was thrust into jail, where
he remained for long, weary months.   It looked as if

his dream were going to come to nothing. But by and by we find him writing a letter from a prison cell in Rome. In this letter we read this heartening word, "I would have you know that the things which happened unto me have fallen out rather unto the furtherance of the gospel." That is, the very things that seemed destined to thwart him had made possible the realization of his hope.

On his way over to Rome there was a terrible storm at sea. This storm raged till all hope of reaching land was destroyed. But instead of its bringing Paul to a grave in the sea, it gave him a place in the confidence and in the hearts of his fellow voyagers that he could have attained in no other way. Then this man was pierced by a thorn. Just what it was we do not know. We do know that he insistently went to God about it and asked for its removal. But the Lord refused his request, saying, "My grace is sufficient for thee." And Paul lived to thank God even for this thorn. "Most gladly, therefore, will I rather glory in my infirmities, that the power of Christ may rest upon me." So constantly did Paul find his losses changed to gain that, after long experimentation in the laboratory of life, he reached this conclusion: "We know that all things work together for good to them that love God."

2. Then if we would capitalize our calamities it will help us to recognize the fact that not every sorrow that comes to us is in accordance with the will of God. For instance, we used to say at every funeral, "Foras-

much as it hath pleased Almighty God, in his wise providence, to take out of this world the soul of," etc. Now, at times this was an altogether fitting word. But at other times it was sheerest mockery and little less than a slander against God. Think of saying such a word over that little child who died the other day of partial starvation in this land of overproduction. Such untimely deaths are not according to the will of God, but flatly contradictory to his will. There are many ills we suffer that are equally so. Then why does not God prevent them? we ask desperately. Because in consistency he cannot, is the only fair answer. He has left us free. Therefore, if we are minded to do wrong, God cannot prevent it.

But, because we so often fail to recognize this, we sometimes blame God for wrongs against which he burns with far greater indignation than we ourselves. When Joseph's life fell into ruins how easy it would have been for him to become bitter and to have flung away from God. But it was his salvation that he was wise enough to see that God was not to blame for the wrongs that he had suffered at the hands of men. How unjust it would have been for him to have railed against God for what those hostile to God had done! How unjust it is of ourselves! We may have suffered desperate wrong at the hands of some member of the Church, or at the hands of some minister of the gospel. But we must not blame God for wrongs that wound him far worse than they wound ourselves.

3. Then it will help us to remember that while God cannot prevent much of the evil that we suffer, yet whether our trouble comes in accordance with his will or contrary to his will, if we remain true, he will bring us through with honor. Not only so, but he will make us the richer for our very losses. This was the experience of this ancient psalmist. It has been the experience of countless others. "You meant it unto me for evil," said Joseph, speaking of the awful wrong he had suffered; "but God meant it unto good." He always does. Nothing can defeat us except our own rebellion. Joseph refused to rebel. Therefore his path of pain became a roadway to abiding spiritual wealth. Such will surely be the goal of your weary road, if, in spite of all your perplexing troubles, you walk it in the fellowship of Christ.

What a Master is ours! What a gospel we have to preach! There is absolutely nothing that can wreck us so long as we live within the circle of His will. With the storms of life beating upon our faces, with disease preying upon our bodies, with ghastly death wrenching our treasures from our clinging fingers, we can still be undismayed. We can shout with Paul, "We know that all things work together for good to them that love God." All things, the joyful things and the bitter things, the things that make us sob and the things that make us sing, the things that seem to impoverish and the things that enrich, all things work together for good. I know there are times when we cannot possibly understand how this can be true. But if in spite of difficulties we hold fast to this high faith, then be sure that one day we, too, shall be able to sing with this psalmist, "It is good for me to have been in trouble."

II

FACING THE FUTURE

(A New Year's Sermon)

Psalm 23: 1

"The Lord is my Shepherd; I shall not want."

I

THIS is the first Sunday of the New Year. I am
sure that we desire to face our untried to-morrow with
calm confidence and hope. It is to help us toward this
great achievement that I have chosen these heartening
words. They are a part of the most familiar song in
all the Bible. More than that, they are a part of the
most familiar song in the literature of the world. Of
all the poems that, through the ages, have been born
in the hot hearts of men of genius, this is the best
known and the best loved. More of you can quote it
from memory than any other single passage in God's
Word. Some of us learned it at mother's knee during
the tender years of childhood. Others came to it in
later life under the stress of heavy burdens and of
compelling needs, or under the spell of a newborn
love for the Good Shepherd. But whenever we came,
whether in joy or sorrow, youth or age, more have

found their way to it and have taken it into their hearts
than any other song that was ever sung.

Naturally, therefore, I do not count on your interest
in what I shall have to say because of the novelty of
my text. I rather count on it for the opposite reason.
I know that familiarity is said to breed contempt.
This is often the case. It might be possible for some
of us to dwell so long beside the sea that we should
cease to wonder at its majesty and mystery. It might
be possible to live under the very shadow of towering
mountains till we no longer lift our eyes to those awful
heights that shimmer under their ermine mantles of
eternal whiteness. But familiarity does not always
breed contempt. Sometimes it leads to a finer appreciation and to a more abiding love. Suppose, for
instance, that next summer you and I should visit
together the farm where I spent my boyhood. I might
say to you, "Here is the winding path that leads down
to my favorite spring. Let us go there and drink."
"O, no," you might answer, "that old spring is so
familiar to you. Let us seek one that you have never
seen before. Let us find a new spring and drink from
that. You will enjoy it so much more." "By no
means," I should answer. "I know this spring is most
familiar. I have visited it with some dear hearts that
to-day sleep on that sunny hillside yonder. I have sat
beside it and had its musical prattle mingle with the
voices of my youthful dreams. But that makes me all
the more eager to visit it again. As I kiss that well-

loved spring upon the lips I shall not only drink refreshing water, but I shall drink tender and precious
memories as well!

So it is with this ageless song. The fact that we
know it so well makes us love it the more. For some
of us it is intimately associated with scenes unspeakably
dear and tender. As we listen to it, we hear again the
cadences of dear voices that are hushed to-day and feel
again the caress of loved hands that have turned to dust.
If this Psalm could write its own biography, what a
thrilling story it would have to tell! There is no sea
that it has not crossed, no land it has not visited, no
road that it has not traveled. It has been thumbed by
beggars and kings, by little children and silver-haired
pilgrims. White-souled mothers have rejoiced over it,
and sinsick harlots have clung to it as their one hope.
Sheltered souls have sung it amidst the peace of God's
house and in the warmth and glow of the home fire-
side. Tempest-tossed souls have also sung it as they
were being pounded by the fists of persecution, or as
they were braving the heartbreak of lonely exile. Dying
saints, surrounded by loved faces, have found it a soft
pillow upon which to rest as they slipped into their last
sleep. Martyrs have found in it calm and comfort as
they went to meet God in winding sheets of flame.

Sometime ago I was called to see a mother who was
very near the sunset. When I reached the home I
found it already under the solemn hush of death. "We
are glad you came," said the daughter softly. "But I

am not sure that mother will know you.   She no longer
seems to recognize any of us."   But I went in and sat
beside her.   How still she was and how altogether indifferent to the sights and sounds of this world!   Then
I put my lips close to her ear and quoted these immortal words, "The Lord is my Shepherd; I shall not want.
He maketh me to lie down in green pastures: he leadeth
me beside the still waters.   He restoreth my soul."
And the dying head nodded a bit, and the thin lips broke
into a smile as if she were seeing old loved faces and
hearing gentle voices wooing she could not resist.
When she had become deaf even to the call of her own
child, she still seemed responsive to the tender appeal of
the Good Shepherd.

We cannot say with authority who wrote these deathless words.   For long centuries they have been credited
to David, the shepherd king.   If he wrote them, as I
assume he did, they were not written, I feel sure, in the
springtime of his life, nor yet in the vigor of midsummer.   These are the words of a man who has lived
much and thought much, who has greatly sinned and
has been greatly forgiven.   He has now reached life's
December, but June is still in his heart.   There he is in
his palace in the city of Jerusalem.   Memory takes him
by the hand and leads him into a far-off yesterday.   His
thin white hair suddenly becomes the golden locks of
youth, his palace roof lifts and overarches into the deep
blue of a cloudless Syrian sky; his scepter becomes a
shepherd's crook, his court and subjects become a flock

of sheep. How familiar is this flock! He knows them every one by name. He knows their peculiarities. Here is one that wears a scar. He has had to rescue him from the jaws of a lion. Here is another that had a veritable genius for getting lost. More than one sleepless night has he spent in the wilds of the hills in search of that foolish sheep. As he looks upon this scene there comes a new warmth to his heart and a new tenderness into his face. "I, too, have a Shepherd," he murmurs. "There is One who has loved me and has sought me in all my wanderings. There is One whose gentleness has made me great, and that One is God. The Lord is my Shepherd; I shall not want."

II

What an amazing discovery! Look at the incredible wealth of it.

1. He dares to claim God as his very own. He does not say that the Lord is a Shepherd. That would have been a wonderful discovery. But one might say that without having any "glowing coal" at his heart. One cannot say "The Lord is my Shepherd," however, without getting a handclasp of life. Luther was right when he said experiential religion is in the personal pronouns. Everything wears a different look when we can speak of it as our very own. Here is a group of women clustered about a cradle. In that cradle is a beautiful, healthy, kicking baby, trying to swallow now its hand, and now its foot. All the women are interested, but

there is one who looks at that little bundle of life with different eyes from the rest. The other women say, "That is a baby!" This one, with eyes lighted by the sweet radiance of mother-love, says, "That is my baby."

"The world grows green on a thousand hills,
  By a thousand rivers the bees are humming,
And a million birds on a million rills,
  Sing of the golden season's coming.
But gazing out on the sun-kissed lea
  And hearing the thrush and the bluebird singing,
I feel that the summer is all for me,
  And all for me the joy it is bringing."

So it may be with the summer time of the soul. We may have God for our very own.

2. Having dared to claim God as his own, the psalmist's next word is the most logical ever uttered. It is the very acme of common sense. If the Lord is my Shepherd, what follows as naturally as night follows day? Just this, "I shall not want." He is able to supply all our needs, and there is none other who can. Soon or late grim want breaks by all other defenses and lays its torturing hands upon us. We are accustomed to say that money talks, and that is true within certain narrow limits; but, in the presence of the deep wants of the heart, it is as dumb as the frozen lips of death. "Knowledge is power," we say. But if it is knowledge that is only of the earth earthly, then in the presence of life's supreme needs it is utter weakness.

It leaves us at last in a more desperate plight than was the hungry prodigal by the swine trough of the far country. Love and friendship are blessings of unspeakable value, but not even these are able to satisfy the deepest hungers of the heart. There is but one way to avoid gaunt and ghastly want, and only one, that is to be able to sing with this glad-hearted poet, "The Lord is my Shepherd."

III

What are some of the wants that the Good Shepherd will supply?

1. If the Lord is our Shepherd, we shall not want for rest and refreshment. We shall surely find in him satisfaction for the hungers and thirsts of our souls. "He maketh me to lie down in green pastures." The sheep lie down because their hunger has been satisfied and because, thanks to the presence of the shepherd, they feel secure. And the same Good Shepherd meets our needs. "I am the bread of life," he declares. "He that cometh to me shall never hunger; and he that believeth on me shall never thirst." With supreme confidence he asserts his ability to satisfy the longing soul. Then he claims also to meet the need of our weary hearts for rest. He stands in our presence to-day as he stood long centuries ago, crying after us as we go our feverish and fear-filled ways: "Come unto me, all ye that labor and are heavy laden, and I will give you rest. Take my yoke upon you, and learn of me; for

I am meek and lowly in heart: and ye shall find rest
unto your souls." The years ahead may disappoint us
in a thousand ways, but it will certainly not disappoint
us in our quest for rest if only the Lord is our Shepherd.

2. With the Lord as our Shepherd, we shall not want
for leadership and guidance. "He leadeth me beside
still waters." That means that he goes before us into
our unknown to-morrow. We have not passed this
way before. No one has. "We are the first that ever
burst into this silent Sea." But this is our consolation,
that our way is not new or strange to him who goes before us. One has called attention to the fact that the
old geographers, after they had mapped the known
world, wrote upon the seas that lay beyond the confines
of the known such words as these: "Here be dragons.
Here be demons that devour men." But the author of
the one hundred and thirty-ninth Psalm had a more
sunny faith. He believed that it was not dragons and
demons that were waiting for us beyond the known, but
that God was there. "If I take the wings of the morning, and dwell in the uttermost parts of the sea; even
there shall thy hand lead me, and thy right hand shall
hold me." Such also was the faith of this shepherd
king. Such may be our faith. Whatever lies beyond
to-day, we may be sure of this, that God is there. He
always goes before.

Not only does the Good Shepherd go before us, but
he gives us guidance. "He leadeth [or guideth] me in

the paths of righteousness." How we need such guidance! How limited is our vision! How often we stand bewildered at the forks of the road not knowing which way to turn! Is there One who does know and who is willing to guide? We sing, "Lead, Kindly Light, amid the encircling gloom." But is there really a Kindly Light that does lead those who are willing to be lead? This psalmist, speaking out of his own experience, says there is. These Scriptures say there is. "When he, the Spirit of Truth is come, he will guide you." The choicest of the saints through the centuries speak to the same purpose. They are sure that the gracious God who guides even the birds in their quest for unfading springtime will not leave his own children to go their unchartered ways in the dark. Therefore, watching the waterfowl in his flight, they sing,

"He who from zone to zone guides through the trackless heavens
    thy solemn flight,
In the long way that I must go alone will guide my steps aright."

He will guide us in our quest for our life's work. He will show us the particular way in which he has planned that we use our lives. He will give us the high joy of looking from our task into his face and saying, "To this end was I born, and for this cause came I into the world." He will also guide us day by day, giving us to know, with Saint Paul, both the constraint and the restraint of the Holy Spirit. He will enable us to say with a conviction born of experience, "In all thy ways acknowledge him, and he shall direct thy path."

3. With the Lord as our Shepherd we may hope for restoration. "He restoreth my soul." This word "restore" has two possible meanings. It means to bring back to health and strength one who is sick. This Good Shepherd of ours claims emphatically to be able to cure the sinsick soul. All the saints are firmly sure of the truthfulness of his claim. To them, for any man to go day after day groaning under the burden of his disease and missing the joys of health seems the height of madness. We hear one of them asking in utter amazement, "Is there no balm in Gilead? is there no physician there?" Why then is there torturing sickness where there might be buoyant and abounding health? Regardless of the deadliness of the disease from which I may have suffered yesterday or from which I may be suffering to-day, there is healing for me at the hands of the Good Shepherd if I will only give him the chance for which he so eagerly yearns.

Then to restore means to seek that which is lost and to bring it back to the fold. Surely David is here speaking out of his own experience. He is thinking of that blackest and most tragic crises of his life. What a crime was his! First, adultery, then murder, not in the heat of passion, but deliberate and cold blooded. Yet even then God did not give him up. He never left off seeking till he found him. That gives hope for you and me. Even yet, after all our defeats and failures, we may win. This year that is ahead need not be simply another year. It may be a new year, new because we ourselves have become new. I know that to some this sounds a bit far away and impossible. We have given up hope of ever being greatly different from what we are. We are not satisfied with the lean, drab lives that we are living, yet we see little chance of ever changing them for the better. When we hear our fellows making New Year's resolutions we smile wistfully or cynically at the sheer futility of it all. We realize how quickly acts become habits and how habits harden into character that is very stubborn and hard to make over. Therefore we say with sad approval:

> "At thirty man suspects himself a fool;
> Knows it at forty, and reforms his plan;
> At fifty chides his infamous delay,
> Pushes his prudent purpose to resolve;
> In all the magnanimity of thought
> Resolves; and re-resolves; then dies the same."

But here is one who stands in a world grown old and gray and shouts, "Old things are passed away; behold they are become new." This is true because "he restoreth my soul."

4. With the Lord as our Shepherd we shall not want for companionship and comfort in sorrow. The Good Shepherd leads us in green pastures and beside the still waters. But the whole journey does not lie among such lovely pastoral scenes. The road changes at times with bewildering suddenness from green pastures to wild and

eerie moors, or to rugged and flinty uplands, or to deep valleys of horror and gloom. But our Shepherd does not forsake us in these desperate hours. He draws the closer to us. "Yea, though I walk through the valley of the shadow of death, I will fear no evil: for thou art with me; thy rod and thy staff they comfort me." He not only walks with us in the darkness, he also brings us through it. Recently I was making a journey by train through a country of wild and rugged beauty. The landscape on every side was gorgeously green and flooded with a golden glory of sunshine. Suddenly it became dark as blackest midnight. As I tried to look through the car windows I could see nothing at all. But in spite of this seeming tragedy I was not afraid. I knew we had entered a tunnel. I knew that this tunnel was not a terminus, but a thoroughfare, that therefore we would soon pass into the sunlight again. Even so the Good Shepherd will not leave us in the dark valley. He will bring us through it into the sunshine. "Weeping may endure for a night, but joy cometh in the morning."

5. Finally, with the Lord as our Shepherd, we shall not want for a home at the end of the journey. "Surely goodness and mercy shall follow me all the days of my life; and I shall dwell in the house of the Lord forever." When the sun is set and the day is done, does the shepherd hie him home in the gloaming, leaving the sheep to shift as best they can in the wilderness through the long night? By no means. It is when the night

comes on that their danger is greatest and that they need him most. Therefore, when he turns his steps home he leads the flock after him and never rests till every one of them is safe within the fold. And may we not expect as much from the Good Shepherd that layeth down his life for the sheep? Will he love us and lead us all through our pilgrimage only to forsake us when our need of him is most desperate? Will he hold our hands in his till we reach that greedy and muddy ditch that we call the grave, and then fling us into it and turn his back upon us forever? I for one cannot believe it. On the contrary, I am very sure that when the evening shadows gather, like the Good Shepherd that he is, he is going to lead us home; that where he is, there we may be also. He loves us too much and has invested too much in us to willingly fling us away.

"For none of the ransomed ever knew
    How deep were the waters crossed,
Nor how dark was the night that the Lord passed through
    Ere he found the sheep that was lost."

III

BLESS THE LORD

(A Thanksgiving Sermon)

Psalm 103: 2

"Bless the Lord, O my soul, and forget not all his benefits."

THIS sane and robust saint has been looking over the
garden of his heart. He has doubtless found many
lovely flowers blooming there. But there is one winsome blossom called gratitude that he does not find
growing in such profusion as he desires. Therefore he
sets himself deliberately to the cultivation of it. He
refuses to allow his soul to become dull and listless and
all but comatose amidst God's amazing mercies. He
refuses to blunder through life, as a blind man might
blunder through an art gallery, never seeing anything
to thrill him or to bring him to his knees in eager
thanksgiving. Therefore he takes himself vigorously
in hand, rouses his drowsy soul into wakefulness by this
urgent appeal, "Bless the Lord, O my soul, and forget
not all his benefits."

I

It is evident that this poet believes that it is a matter
of choice whether we are thankful or thankless. He is

sure that all who really desire to be grateful can be. He knows that just as we can, if we so desire, deliberately cultivate the noxious weeds of hatred, malice, and ingratitude, even so we can cultivate the opposite. No man can keep house with himself with any sort of understanding without realizing that there is no weed so poisonous that he cannot grow it in the soil of his own soul. But this is equally true: There is no rare flower of the spirit too lovely or too beautiful for us to grow in that same amazing soil. Therefore, if we wish to cultivate this fine flower of gratitude, we can, regardless of what our circumstances may be. But if this is the case, how are we to go about it? There is something more involved in it than a mere saying of "Thank you" to those here and there who do us favors. It is well to say this both to God and man, but we may do so, and yet be very poor in real gratitude. Our thanksgiving is too often from the lips only. But if it is to be of any real worth, it must be from the heart. And how may we be grateful in our hearts? We can do so, says our poet, by refusing to be so forgetful. "Forget not all his benefits"—mark you, he does not ask that we remember them all. His request is very modest. He merely asks that we not forget them all. "Think," he says, "and then you will thank." The reason we are so thankless is because we are so thoughtless. No wonder that Bunyan, with his fine spiritual insight, picked out Forgetful Green as the most dangerous bit of road between the City of Destruction and

Mount Zion. Its very greenness is born of the millions of mercies that are buried there with no shaft of gratitude to mark their resting place.

II

But if we are to think in order to thank, what must be the nature of our thinking? What is it that this wise singer urges us so earnestly to remember? As we look over the list we shall find that the very things that some of us cling to most tenaciously and brood over most often are left out altogether.

For instance, he does not tell us to think upon our enemies, those uncouth and grouchy souls that rub us the wrong way and get onto our nerves generally. Nor does he tell us to brood over our petty slights and injuries. What a fatal facility some have for missing all the music of life because their ears are so attentive to the discords! I recall a young lady of this kind who once boarded in our home. Seldom did she come to dinner in the evening that she did not have a story to tell of some petty annoyance or wrong that she had suffered during the day. If ever anyone did her a kindness, she kept it a secret. If she found a lovely rose bush in bloom by her path, she utterly forgot the roses. She never plucked one of them to wear over her heart, but she never failed to gather the thorns to wear, not over her heart, but in it. Of course she was not greatly given to gratitude.

Neither does the psalmist urge us to think only of the

benefits that have come to others and contrast them with the seeming inferiority of our own. How easy it is for us to persuade ourselves that our neighbor is getting the better of it, finding life far fuller than ourselves. There was once a dog, you remember, that had been out foraging. He had been very successful. He was coming home with a large piece of meat in his mouth, and possibly a bit of gratitude in his canine heart. But as he was crossing a lovely, clear stream upon a footlog, he saw the reflection of himself in the water. And what a piece of meat that other dog had! It was so much larger and better than his own that he at once threw his away in order to dive headlong after the piece that belonged to the other dog. The end of it all was that he came home empty handed with a grudge on life for robbing him of that of which he had really robbed himself. Surely the wise man was right when he said, "The eyes of a fool are in the ends of the earth." He is so busy in looking at the things of others that he despises what is his own.

The way of gratitude, then, says our wise poet, is not to catalogue what we have not, but what we have. We are to think on his benefits, to remember God's gracious gifts to ourselves. The flowers growing by our door may seem a bit meager at times, but there are always enough to make a lovely bouquet of gratitude if we only remember to gather them. We never realize our own wealth till we take time enough to think upon it instead of looking enviously at that of others. Did

you ever hear of the House with the Golden Windows?
A lad lived, so the story runs, in a lovely little cottage
upon the side of a mountain that overlooked a beautifully wooded valley. Away on the other side of the
valley stood another house so much more wonderful
than the one in which he lived that he soon ceased to be
grateful for his own, but rather to despise it. For this
house across the valley had golden windows. Often he
would look at them in the light of the early morning sun
and resolve that, as soon as he was old enough, he would
leave his own commonplace house, and hie him away to
the house with the golden windows. At last the long-
looked-for day came. He made the toilsome journey
and arrived, in the late afternoon, at the spot where he
thought the wonderful house stood. But he did not
find it. He found instead one that was more ordinary,
by far, than his own. He was sure there was a mistake
somewhere; so, seeing a girl playing in the yard, he
asked her if she knew where was the House with the
Golden Windows. "Indeed, I do," she replied eagerly.
And she pointed to his own house across the valley,
whose windows were at that moment a blaze of golden
glory. And he saw for the first time the beauty of what
was his own, and hurried back to it with grateful
heart. And you and I, too, live in a house with golden
windows if we only had eyes to see. For our windows
are made golden by the shining of the Son of Righteousness who has risen upon us with healing in his
beams.

III

What, then, are some of the benefits, the remembrance of which the poet felt sure would beget within our hearts the fine grace of gratitude? He does not mention our day-by-day mercies that we often come to regard as commonplace because they are so constant. He does not mention the splendor of the sunrise, the ordered coming of the seasons, the bloom of flowers, the song of birds, the handclasps of friends, the tender love of the home circle. In the realization that every good and every perfect gift is from above, in the faith that possessing God we possess all else, he passes at once to the benefits that have come directly from his hands. And what are these? We shall not undertake to name them all, nor shall we follow the order followed by our psalmist.

1. He thanks God for the revelation that he has made of himself through Moses and through his own personal experience. And it is absolutely amazing how fully this man has come to know God, in spite of the fact that he lived long centuries before Jesus came to gather little children into his arms and to take upon his shoulders the burdens of every nameless and needy soul, and to say to us, "God is like me; he that hath seen me, hath seen the Father."

2. He is thankful for the infinite beauty of God that this revelation has disclosed. How winsome he has found him to be! How altogether lovely and lovable!

No wonder his soul falls upon its knees in spontaneous thanksgiving as he thinks upon such gracious qualities as these:

(1) God is like a father. "Like as a father pitieth his children, so the Lord pitieth them that fear him." And how far fuller is this truth declared to us through Jesus Christ! He tells that the tenderest love of the tenderest father is only a most dim and blurred copy of the love of God. He tells of a certain graceless boy who ran away from his father's house, ran past his own wealth, both physical and spiritual, ran past his friends, ran past his decency and self-respect; but he could never run past his father's love. He was always missing him, always longing for him, always watching with yearning unspeakable for his return.

(2) God's heart, being that of a father, is of necessity a forgiving heart. "Who forgiveth all thine iniquities." Nor does he do so in a niggardly and grudging fashion, but abundantly and eagerly. "He is plenteous in mercy." He is always doing things on a grand scale. When he wants space, he pushes back its boundaries to infinity. When he wants stars, he sows them heaven-wide. When he wants flowers, he colors every hill and valley with their beauty. When he forgives, he does so grandly, forgiving literally all our iniquities and removing them as far from us as is the east from the west.

Then this plenteous forgiveness means also that he takes us back into his confidence, trusts us as if we had always been true. In fact, if we may credit that infinitely lovely disclosure made to Jeremiah, he actually forgets that we ever sinned. "He will forgive their iniquity, and will remember their sin no more." This is the only something in all the universe that God ever forgets. He never forgets the least of his children. He never forgets their efforts to serve him. He remembers with infinite appreciation. But he does forget our sin. He turns his back upon it and invites us to do the same. He takes us fully into his bracing confidence, saying even to the weakest of us, "Go and sin no more."

3. He is thankful because in God he has found the secret of unfailing youth. "Thy youth is renewed like the eagle's." In all ages men have hated to grow old. I have known some to grow old only the faster because of their frantic efforts to fight it off. Now, I believe we should remain young physically as long as we can. But fight against it how we may, this house we live in is sure to fall into ruins. No beauty secrets, no surgery, no mystic fountain of youth can prevent it. Winter is certain to come to our bodies, but in spite of that we can have abiding springtime in our hearts. In a church of which I was once pastor there was a man loaded with some fourscore years. In addition to this, he carried the burden of heavy sorrows and dear dreams that never came true. But never once did I hear him complain or utter one word of discouragement. Whenever he came into a meeting, large or small, it was like

turning on a light. It was like opening a window that let in a breeze fresh from sun-kissed mountains and sweet with the odor of June flowers. He shared with our poet the secret of unfailing youth.

4. Finally, he is thankful because, in a world of restlessness and weariness, of broken hearts and broken hopes, he has found One who can abidingly satisfy. "Who satisfieth," he sings gratefully. What shall it profit a man if he gain the whole world, and misses him who alone can satisfy? What have we lost if we miss the things for which men are scrambling most madly and find real satisfaction? On the west coast of England there is the grave of a man who while he lived, moved about his community like a rich and rare perfume. His tomb bares upon it this inscription, "Here lies ——, a man who was satisfied with Jesus." If that can be truly said of us, we have sufficient to make all time and eternity one great thanksgiving day.

IV

As this radiant singer thought on these benefits, his heart naturally grew big with gratitude. But he knew that to be grateful in his own heart was not enough. This was the first step; but a second was absolutely essential, and that was giving expression to his gratitude.

1. This is good for the one who is grateful. To keep such a rare treasure shut up in our hearts is to lose it. No flower needs the sun any more than the sweet flower

of gratitude. As we give it away, it is not only as unwasting as Elisha's cruse of oil, it even increases the more we share it.

2. Then we ought to give expression to our gratitude because it heartens those to whom we are grateful. And how desperately do some need heartening! I used to think, when I was quite a young preacher, that what the average man most needed was "a good skinning." But I have long since learned my mistake. What folks need most is a little encouragement, a little something to let them know that their efforts, however blundering, are recognized and appreciated. How far more smoothly the machinery of life would run, both in the home and out of it, if it were oiled a little more frequently and freely by that fine lubricant called gratitude. One day, I fear, we shall speak into ears that do not hear any more, words of appreciation that, if we only spoke now, would put a new elasticity into the step, a glad sparkle into the eye, and plant fresh roses upon the cheek. Why are we so grudging with a treasure whose sharing would so enrich both him who gives and him who receives?

3. Finally, we ought to give expression to our thanks because by so doing we gladden the heart of God. One tells of a certain tired minister who, on a late Saturday afternoon, was trying to finish his Sunday morning sermon. His interruptions had been many and his nerves were on edge from sheer weariness. Then came a knock at his door. He braced himself for another

drain upon his energies and said, "Come in." Then the door was opened to a slit and a little sunny-faced girl looked in. "Daddy, may I come in?" she asked. And when consent was given, she bounded across the room, climbed into the tired man's lap and began to caress him in her sweet childish fashion. And then she said, "Daddy, I didn't come to ask you for a thing. I just came to climb into your lap and hug your neck and kiss your lips and tell you what a good, kind, sweet daddy you are." And so much warmth slipped into his tired heart that it crowded out all the weariness. And God is a Father, and his heart, too, warms at our giving of thanks. Therefore, "Let the redeemed of the Lord say so."

IV

A CRY FROM THE CROSS

(A COMMUNION SERMON)

Psalm 22: 1; Matthew 27: 46

"My God, my God, why hast thou forsaken me?"

THESE words come to us out of a long gone past.
We first hear them from the lips of this ancient psalmist whose name has been forgotten for many centuries.
But he was doubtless not the first to utter them. They
have been either articulate or inarticulate upon the lips
of countless millions of perplexed men and women as
the years have come and gone. Who among us has
gotten very far into life without having had wrung
from us this tearful cry? This is a question that has
literally sobbed its way through the centuries. It is in
a sense an outcry of the race. It is as old as man. It is
as new as the pain of your own broken heart.

But as intensely human as is this question, we are
thoroughly startled to find it upon the lips of our Lord.
Yet as he hangs on the cross he takes these words from
this ancient psalmist and makes them the vehicle for the
expression of his agony. After terrible hours of suffering he flings out this age-old question, "My God, my
God, why?" In fact, these words have become his very

46

own. We tend to forget that anyone ever uttered them except him whose was the tenderest heart that was ever broken and whose were the purest lips that ever spoke. Surely it is our Lord who has given to these words their immortality. Let us think of them, then, not so much as those of a long dead poet, but rather as the exceedingly bitter cry of the dying Son of God. Of course, we cannot hope to comprehend them. We can only pray that our imperfect glimpses may bring to us some spiritual enrichment.

I

Upon the lips of Jesus these words have two striking peculiarities.

1. Here Jesus addresses the Infinite by a name that he has never used in speaking to him before, nor does he ever use it afterwards. When he flings out this question he addresses the Eternal as "God." "My God, my God," he cries. Now, the one word that he uses in speaking to God everywhere else is "Father." This, too, is the name by which he most often speaks of God. When we hear him for the first time in the temple as a lad of twelve, he says, "Wist ye not that I must be about my Father's business?" When he teaches us to pray he tells us to say "Our Father." When he would enforce upon us the reasonableness of prayer he does so by reminding us of the fact that God is our Father. "If ye then, being evil, know how to give good gifts unto your children, how much more shall your Father

which is in heaven give good things to them that ask
him?" The first word he utters upon the cross is
"Father, forgive them, for they know not what they
do." When the ghastly fight is over his last word
is, "Father, into thy hands I commend my spirit."
Almost constantly did Jesus call God "Father" in speaking of him. Always and everywhere he did so when
speaking to him, except here. Only here does he say
"My God."

2. Then this text upon the lips of Jesus is peculiar
because it is a question that he addresses to God. This
is the only question, so far as the record goes, that
Jesus ever asked God during his entire earthly ministry.
We are full of questions. Jesus questioned only once.
There were, of course, times of conflict. There were
times when he looked at the will of God not without
amazement that his Father could so choose for him.
But always he accepted that will without question. He
never faltered in his faith that the Father's plan for him
was the best plan. Near the beginning of his ministry
he said in reply to a suggestion from his mother, "Mine
hour is not yet come." By this he meant to say,
"Henceforth the finger that points to the hour that I am
to act and the task that I am to do will be that of no
human hand. It will be that of my Father." At the
end of the journey he prayed, "If it be possible, if there
is any other way, let this cup pass from me. Nevertheless not as I will, but as thou wilt." But here Jesus
flings out a question.

II

What does this question on the part of Jesus indicate?

1. It indicates a sense of forsakenness. Jesus, for the moment at least, has lost his vivid realization of the Divine Presence. His Father seems no longer so real as he has been in other days. Remember that Jesus up to this time had lived his life in the most perfect realization of the presence of God. What the greatest of the saints have experienced at the transfiguration moments of their lives, Jesus experienced continuously. To him God was always the supreme reality. To him he was always closer than breathing and nearer than hands and feet. How confidently he speaks of this intimate association. "He that hath sent me is with me: the Father hath not left me alone; for I do always those things that please him." When near the end of his journey he said to his disciples with great sadness, "It shall come to pass that ye shall be scattered, every man to his own, and shall leave me alone." Then he corrected himself, "Yet I am not alone. The Father is with me." But now that Presence that has been his very life seems to have withdrawn from him so that the deepest darkness he has ever known closes over him.

2. This cry also indicates perplexity. God's strange ordering of things left him baffled and bewildered. For mark you, this question is intensely real. Jesus never degenerated into a mere actor. In everything he did there was always perfect sincerity. When he prayed he did not pray simply to set us an example. He prayed

because prayer was for him an absolute necessity. He could not keep spiritually fit without it. When he was tempted his temptation was a reality. If this is not the case, then his conflicts can be of no help to us. They only mock us. In the battles that we have to fight we are capable of being wounded. In the battles that we have to fight we may utterly lose our souls. If such is not the case with our Master, then his struggles are worth less than nothing to us. Jesus asked this question because he was sorely perplexed.

3. This question is born of a terrible agony. There was the agony of a dimmed realization of God. There was the agony of bewilderment. There was the agony of physical suffering. The cross was the most horrible torture that the fiendish ingenuity of man ever devised. But the physical agony of our Lord was as nothing in comparison with his spiritual suffering. It was this that broke his heart. It was this that wrung from him this terrible question that sounds so little like the shout of a victor and so much like the wail of one whose dreams, instead of coming true, have only led him into the quagmire of desolation and death. "My God, why?" This question was born of immeasurable heartache.

III

Now it is easy for us to understand a less vivid realization of God on the part of ourselves. It is easy for us to understand perplexity and agony on the part of ourselves. But how are we to account for these in Jesus Christ our Lord? It is not surprising that we sometimes have this question wrung from our lips, but how can we account for it upon the lips of him who said, "He that hath seen me hath seen the Father"? Of course, we cannot hope fully to answer this question. At best we can but dimly grope.

But of this at least we may be sure. The agony, the perplexity, the sense of forsakenness on the part of Jesus was not due to his consciousness of the anger of God. He had no such consciousness. The old idea that God the Father was flinging the thunderbolts of his wrath at his Son is to us unthinkable. God was never more pleased with Jesus than when he hung on the cross. Let us never forget the love of Jesus for men is also the love of God. Jesus on the cross is God on the cross. "God was in Christ reconciling the world unto himself." The perplexity and pain therefore that wrung this cry from Jesus was certainly not born of any anger or displeasure on the part of God the Father.

No more are we to assume that because Jesus uttered this bewildered and agonized question. His faith had been shattered by the torture through which he was passing. While his realization of God is not so vivid as at other times, his faith in God is still firm, triumphant, and strong. Therefore he does not lapse into sullen silence. He believes that there is One who sees and understands all that he suffers. He believes that there is One who is able and willing to make all things clear.

He believes that God still lives. Not only so, but he dares to claim this God as his very own. In spite of his bitter agony he cries, "My God." Then he proceeds to bring his perplexity up before him and fling it down at his feet in the faith that he doeth all things well.

Why then this sense of loss and bewilderment on the part of our Lord? We find at least some light on the question, I think, in this fact, that such bewilderment is inevitable if he is to be fully identified with ourselves. The Word has become flesh. Jesus is one with us. "Wherefore in all things it behooved him to be made like unto his brethren." Now since he shares our nature, he must also share our perplexities. And we have them, God knows. Strange and bewildering sorrows often overwhelm us and we cry, "Why?" There are times when the pastor has this question flung at him till he is heartsick with the bleak tragedy of it all. There are those present even now who are asking it through lips that are white and drawn with pain.

What answer can we make to these perplexed and distressed souls? What have we to offer baffled men and women who stand face to face with veils through which they cannot see, and grim doors to which they find no key? Well, we have this at least: We can offer a marvelous Saviour who has walked just their road and who is, therefore, able to enter into full sympathy with them. "For in that he himself hath suffered being tempted, he is able to succor them that are tempted." We can assure them that our Christ is not angry with them because they question. He himself said "Why?" We can assure them further that this Christ of ours, when he was perplexed, brought his perplexity to God and that God did not fail him, but brought him through in triumph. Then we can add with superb confidence this crowning word: This undestanding Christ is infinitely able and infinitely eager to do the same for them, even the weakest.

Finally this agony of bewilderment and perplexity on the part of our Lord is the natural outcome of his identification with us in our sin. He is the Lamb of God that taketh away the sin of the world. There on the cross he is being wounded for our transgressions and bruised for our iniquities. There for love's sake he who knew no sin is being made to be sin for us. Now since he shares with us the burden of our guilt, it is not only natural but inevitable that he should feel that sense of forsakenness that comes from the bearing of such a burden. His agonizing bewilderment is born of his sharing the desolation of the sheep that had gone astray. No wonder then that he cries, "My God, my God, why hast thou forsaken me?" But his very suffering wins us. Lifted upon the cross, he draws all men unto himself. Therefore his cry of agony and seeming defeat becomes a shout of victory. From this skull-shaped hill of grimest failure he marches to the conquest of the world.

V

HE SHALL PROSPER

Psalm 1: 3

"In whatsoever he doeth, he shall prosper."

I

"HE shall prosper"—surely here is a word to bring us to our feet at eager attention. This psalmist is undertaking to point us to the path of prosperity. He is offering us a recipe for success. His message is, therefore, of vital interest. Everybody desires to succeed; nobody wishes to fail. In fact, we have very little time or patience for failures. But we are ever ready to honor those who have made good. Ours is in a peculiar sense a generation of success worshipers. Nor are our ideas of success always the highest. We do not always give first place to those whose prosperity is in the realm of the spiritual. We rather give it to those whose success is purely of the earth earthly. Worse still, we often do this regardless of the price that these may have paid for their success. It may have been won at the price of their own honor. But caught under the spell of their winnings, we pass over these ugly facts as matters of minor importance. The big thing for us is success.

Now, the good news that this poet has for us is just this: Everybody may prosper. Everybody may be in the truest and highest sense successful. This may be so regardless of whether we succeed or fail as the world counts success and failure. We may invest wisely and have everything we touch turn to gold. We may have a palatial home in the city and a mansion in the mountains or down by the sea. Or we may trust the wrong enterprise or the wrong man and lose the pitiful little pittance that we have been years in piling up. We may have to live in a very humble cottage. Disease may lay its weakening hand upon us and steal away our health. Death may come and rob us of those we love. But in spite of all circumstances, whether good or bad, whether fraught with laughter or with tears, every one who meets the conditions will be in the truest sense successful.

II

What, then, are the conditions of success?

1. The first fact that the psalmist points out is that the road to prosperity is one that is shut within limits. There are certain things that the man who would make a success simply cannot do. This will be disappointing to some. We of to-day are especially impatient of restraints of any kind. We seem to have a veritable passion for doing as we please. But resent it how we may, the way to real success can only be traveled by those who are willing to make certain very definite re-

fusais. The vessel sailing from New York to Liver-
pool must do this or it will never arrive. It will only
become a derelict. The train going from station to
station must do this or it will miss its destination and
become a worthless wreck. Man must do this or life
for him ends in disaster. Esau is a pathetic illustra-
tion of this truth. He did not fail for lack of ability.
His tragedy was that he was a profane man—that is,
his life had no fence round it. He allowed his soul
to become a common. Any cloven-footed devil could
romp across it at his pleasure. Every prosperous life
is circumscribed by certain great refusals.

(1) The man who would make a real success must
refuse to walk in the counsel of the ungodly. Who are
the ungodly? They are the folks who reckon without
God. They do not have to be dishonest or in any way
crooked in their dealings. They do not have to be rakes
or libertines. They may be as decent as decency.
They may be as respectable as respectability. All they
have to do is to ignore God, shut him out of their
thoughts and out of their lives. The ungodly are the
practical atheists, who, though they may recite creeds,
live as if God were only a myth and a dream. To walk
in their counsel is to take their advice and pattern our
lives by theirs. To take this course, says the poet, is
surely to miss success. No one can truly prosper who
stubbornly ignores the facts of life. Certainly no man
can hope for success who ignores the supreme fact
which is God.

(2) The man who would hope for success must refuse to stand in the way of sinners. Standing in the way of sinners marks a lower step than walking in the counsel of the ungodly. The man who is walking may pass beyond the confines of the dominion of the evil in which he finds himself. But to stand denotes a decaying sensitiveness to sin. It indicates that the wrongdoer is losing his antagonism to evil, that on the contrary, he is being brought under its spell. Sin is always progressive. "From what kind of plant would you say those seed came?" said a friend one day to Dr. Chapman as he showed him, in the palm of his hand, some very small seed. "I should think they came from one that was very small, indeed," was the natural answer. "No, you are mistaken," was the reply. "Those seed came from a plant that is three hundred feet in height, thirty-five feet in diameter, and one hundred and five feet in circumference. They came from one of the giant redwood trees of California." Now, the most impressive fact about those little seed was their tremendous growing power. It is ever so with sin. How easily we pass from a thought to a practice, from walking to standing! But in so doing we are surely killing our chances of winning success.

(3) He who would find prosperity must refuse to sit in the seat or assembly of the scornful. To take the scorner's seat is to take the lowest place possible. What is wrong with the scorner? First, he chooses to sit instead of to serve. He persistently refuses to take any

part in the game. He is content to stand on the side lines and watch the struggles of his fellows. The fact that some are losing the fight is no business of his. The fact that some are being sorely wounded, that others are falling under the weight of heavy burdens, concerns him not in the least. The high task of helping to heal the world's open sore is not of the slightest interest to him. "Is not this a needy world?" I ask. "Are there not those to whom you might stretch a steadying hand as they blunderingly walk their weary way?" "Doubtless," he answers. But having answered, he keeps his seat till the day is done and the night is on, and his one big chance has forever slipped through his fingers.

But the fact that the scorner sits does not mean that he is entirely idle. There is one job that he can carry on without ever taking the trouble to rise to his feet. He can play the cynic. He can sneer and snarl and growl. He can bark contemptuously at everything and everybody. And this he does. He laughs at the faith of his childhood. He sneers at the dreams of his young and tender years. He curls his lips at ideals that were once the very jewels of his soul. He smiles upon what would once have filled him with disgust. He looks with lazy tolerance upon wrongs that once would have brought his soul to its feet fire-eyed and eager for battle. Upon all fine enthusiasms, even the holiest and the best, he pours the hot acid of his scorn and contempt.

Then he feels himself especially at home as a critic of his fellows. He knows human nature to perfection. He can see more through a cobwebbed keyhole than others can see through a plate glass window. Therefore he laughs at all high motives, is perfectly sure that every patriot is a demagogue; that every minister, missionary, or Christian worker is either a fool or a hypocrite. Even the love of a mother for her child is only animal instinct and is purely selfish. For him there are no heroes, and the fine gold of goodness is counterfeit and nothing more. So he sits and so he snarls. The longer he sits the more bitter is his snarl, and the more bitterly he snarls the more firmly he becomes fixed in his seat. The two act and react on each other till he becomes a creature so horrible that we read of him with real approval this stern sentence, "Surely God scorneth the scorner." No wonder, therefore, that our poet declares that the man who would make a success of life must shun the seat of the scornful as he would shun the very pits of hell.

2. But there are great positives as well as refusals necessary for him who would find real prosperity. He must not only say no to the wrong, he must say yes to the right. He must not only avoid the seat of the scornful, but his delight must be in the law of the Lord.

(1) The prosperous man reads his Bible. In no other way could he have an intelligent delight in it. There are to-day certain so-called heresies among us that some feel are threatening the destruction of the

Bible. Some fear that it is going to be destroyed by a too liberal interpretation. Others are equally afraid that a too crass and wooden interpretation is going to work its doom. But in my opinion the most dangerous heresy that threatens the Book, for the vast majority, is the heresy of neglect. For the Bible to become a lost book to you and me, it is not necessary that it be discredited and torn into shreds. All that is necessary is for us to lay it carefully, even reverently, upon our center tables and let it alone. This prosperous man refuses to neglect his Bible.

(2) He not only reads his Bible, he delights in it. This he does for many reasons. He finds it truly great literature. But the supreme reason for his delight is in the fact that he finds in it God's message to his own soul. Of course the Bible of the psalmist was nothing like so rich and full as ours. But even in his, he found the treasured experiences of great spiritual pioneers that had gone questing after God and had found him. The poet's joy in the law of the Lord was, therefore, not simply in the fact that he saw in it something beautiful and interesting upon which to look. It was rather that he found in it something through which to look, not into his own heart only, but into the very heart of God. His delight in the Word was, therefore, born of his delight in him who is the inspirer of the Word.

(3) Reading the Bible and delighting in it, he read it more and more. And the more he read it the greater

became his delight. That is ever the case. This amazing Book is one that does not grow old and stale through being read too often or too constantly. Through all the changing years it remains to those who win their way to its heart as fresh as the first rose of June, and as inexhaustible as a gushing spring from the hills. Our prosperous man found it so. His mind became so richly stored with the precious truth of God's Word that this truth came to his mind as spontaneously as the absent faces of those he loved the best. Thus it came to pass that in his law did he meditate day and night. And out of all this came his prosperity.

III

What was the nature of his prosperity?

It was not necessarily success in the winning of things. The psalmist does not say, "Whatsoever he doeth shall prosper." That is not always the case. I have known some very good men to make some very poor investments. But what he does say is, "In whatsoever he doeth, he shall prosper." That is, the man who delights in God and in God's Word shall prosper, regardless of whether the enterprises in which he invests succeed or go to the wall. We read that Joseph prospered. But his prosperity was not simply in the fact that he went from a nomad's tent to a palace on the Nile. This might have worked his everlasting ruin. His real prosperity was not in what he won, but in what he was. So it is with the man who makes God his choice, whether his purse be full or empty; in the wealth that is wealth indeed, he will surely prosper.

1. "He shall be like a tree planted by the rivers of water." The word "planted" implies purpose. The tree is not where it is by mere chance. An intelligent agent has planted it there. As it grows it is fulfilling a purpose. So it is with the prosperous man. He will be able to discern in his own life the outworking of a beautiful plan of God. When he reads, "There was a man sent from God whose name was John," he will not be afraid to substitute his own name for that of the great forerunner. From his task, whether large or small, he will dare to look into God's face and say, "To this end was I born, and for this cause came I into the world, that I might do this bit of work for thee." And any man who can do that is a success.

2. The fact that this man is like a planted tree suggests steadfastness. He is not the plaything of every breeze that blows. He sings with the author of the sixteenth Psalm, "I have set the Lord always before me. Because he is at my right hand I shall not be moved." How we need such stanch men!

"God give us men. The time demands
  Strong minds, great hearts, true faith, and willing hands,
    Men whom the lust of office does not kill;
  Men whom the spoils of office cannot buy;
    Men who possess opinion and a will;
  Men who have honor; men who will not lie."

3. He is rich in usefulness. He "bringeth forth his

fruit in his season." Where he farms the wheat fields grow golden, and the sweet flowers of the spirit, love, joy, peace, long-suffering, gentleness, goodness, and the rest flourish in rich profusion. Where he walks tired hearts in some measure forget their aches and losses and find themselves strangely richer in rest and hope. And when he goes home to God at the end of the day, he leaves for those who knew him best "a lonesome place against the sky."

4. Finally, this prosperous man is rich in the life that abides. "His leaf also shall not wither." What exquisite poetry, yet what sober truth! All the trees of God's planting are evergreens. It was Jerome K. Jerome that taught me to love the evergreen. I remember one that grew on the hillside above our home when I was a boy. It was a veritable poem, yet to see it in the springtime when all the hillside was a riot of color and all the other trees were decking themselves in their Easter garments was not to be greatly impressed. No more was it conspicuous in the noontide of midsummer when every other tree was in full dress. In the autumn when the frost came and decked its fellows in gaudy garments of crimson and gold it looked almost commonplace. But when, a little later, the sharp shears of the winter wind clipped the leaves from the other trees and they waved their bare boughs like the ghastly hands of a skeleton, then it was that the evergreen came into its own. Then even the birds learned that it was good to build their nests in the boughs of the evergreen.

And there are evergreen lives, says Jerome, and in so saying he is but repeating what this psalmist said many centuries before. To make God our choice is to lay hold on abiding springtime, and that is success, now and evermore.

VI

THE TURNING POINT

Psalm 119: 59

"I thought on my ways, and turned my feet unto thy testimonies."

THIS man is giving us a bit of his personal history. He is telling how life for him took on a new departure. He is looking back to a certain yesterday when he entered into possession of that transforming experience which the writers of the New Testament describe as a passing out of death into life. As he looks back to this radiant yesterday there is a warm glow in his heart, there is a joy shining out from his eyes that has grown deeper and sweeter with the passing of the years. "On this day," he declares humbly and gladly, "I thought on my ways and turned, and in turning, came into possession of the peace and power of a great discovery.

Now about the most abidingly interesting something in the world is a human experience. We delight to hear of the struggles and failures and triumphs of men and women like ourselves. But of all human experiences there is none quite so gripping as the experience of a soul with God. Here is a man who has made life's supreme discovery. Here is one who has found his way into the secret place of the Most High. It is a discovery that we ourselves should like to make if we have not done so already.   How did this man come to make it?   How did he find his way to spiritual certainty?   What road did he travel?   Let us find that road that we may plant our wayward feet upon it.

I

When we ask this man the secret of his conversion, when we ask what marked the turning point in his life, he tells us that it was an outcome of his thinking.   All right conduct has its fountain source in right thinking, just as all wrong conduct is born of wrong thinking.   This man was somehow made to think.   It is always a good day in the life of any man when he can be brought to do some straight, honest thinking.   Many of life's supreme tragedies are results, not of our viciousness, not of our cruelty, not of our depravity, but of our thoughtlessness.

> "And yet it was never in my heart
>   To play so ill a part,
>   But evil is wrought for want of thought
>   As well as for want of heart."

How many lives are destroyed every year in America, for instance, by accidents!   We kill more in any single year in this fashion than we lost in the World War.   Now, a large part of these accidents are not necessary at all.   They are the results of sheer carelessness.   They are born of our refusal to think.   We dash madly and thoughtlessly down the street in our cars.

Suddenly there is a crash. Then we think how easily the catastrophe might have been avoided. If we had only been as thoughtful before the tragedy as we have been since, it need never have occurred.

How many fine opportunities we throw away because we refuse to think! How many men do you know who are misfits? They have not chosen their vocations, they have rather been pushed into them by the stern hand of necessity. They are not the least in love with their work, but in their unwelcome grooves they must remain whether they wish it or not. How did it come about? In many instances it was the result of mere thoughtlessness. They trifled with their educational opportunities. They refused to look ahead. They refused to prepare themselves for the doing of any definite task. Through sheer refusal to think they flung away their opportunities, till, by and by, they found themselves weighted with responsibilities. They had to do something and that something turned out to be a task altogether uncongenial. It might have been vastly different if they had only been willing to think.

What pain we often inflict upon others through our thoughtlessness! Sometime ago there were two small boys who found themselves alone with a magnificent wax doll that belonged to their sister. Upon examining the face of that doll they saw that it was made of wax. At once they wondered what kind of chewing gum this would make. So they picked off a piece, tasted it, and found it to their liking. Then they took another. By and by their mouths were crammed with the gum, but the poor doll, while still bravely smiling, looked as if she had had the worst possible case of smallpox. These boys did not intend to make a wreck of the doll. Still less did they intend to wet their sister's face with tears. They were only normal boys that just failed to think.

Years ago I knew a great husky man who married a frail little slip of a girl. He loved her devotedly in his rough uncouth way, but through sheer thoughtlessness he wrecked her health and broke her heart. One day I visited that home when the wife lay close upon the borderland of death. To break the monotony of watching and to secure some fresh water, I took the old-fashioned bucket, for their home was in the country, and went down the winding path to the spring. As I made my way along the narrow trail among the trees I heard a sound that startled me. Turning in the direction from which it came, I saw through the leaves this man upon his knees. He was clinging to a little sapling that shook in the grip of his brawny hands. He was sobbing as I have never heard a strong man sob before or since. "God, I didn't mean to do it! I just didn't think! Give me another chance!" That was the substance of his prayer. I did not disturb him. I could only pass on and leave him with the agony that his own thoughtlessness had brought upon him.

Then how often we wound by our ingratitude!

How many fathers and mothers in our city are learning even now how sharper than a serpent's teeth it is to have a thankless child. Why are we so ungrateful? One big reason is that we are so thoughtless. "Bless the Lord, O my soul," sang a certain psalmist, "and forget not all his benefits." The words "thank" and "think" come from the same Anglo-Saxon root. To refuse to think is to refuse to thank. To be thoughtful is the very first step toward being thankful. Hence, in speaking of certain choice souls we say, "He is so thoughtful," or "She is so thoughtful." And these thoughtful ones are also grateful. Being grateful, they give expression to their gratitude in words and deeds of tenderness and love.

But if our thoughtlessness works havoc in our relationships one with another, it is, if possible, even more deadly in our relation to God. It is so easy to forget God. We even forget each other in spite of the fact that we may clasp hands and look into each other's faces day by day. How much more prone we are to forget our unseen Lord! He does not utter his voice in the streets. He does not strive nor cry. We cannot see him with our physical eyes. In the rush of things, for many, the unseen becomes the unreal. For many, therefore, the fact of God is as dim as the shadow of a dream. But this man tells us that on a certain day of which he could never think without a quicker beating of the heart, he thought, and through his thinking passed out of withered winter into colorful and blooming spring.

II

I wonder what led to his thinking. He does not tell us. We can only guess.

1. He may have been led to think by a sense of the sheer futility of life as he was living it. He found himself in the grip of unsatisfied hungers. He found himself tortured by thirsts that the fountains of this earth had not been able to slake. Tormented by these hungers and thirsts, he began to look about him with inquiring eyes. "I wonder," he said, "if there is anywhere a bread of which, if I eat, I will hunger no more. I wonder if there is anywhere a fountain from which I may drink and find it a well of water springing up into everlasting life?" Possibly, then, he was driven to thinking by an aching void that this world could not fill.

2. He may have been made thoughtful, as we sometimes are, by the bursting upon him of some terrible calamity that left his life in ruins. One day he was passing along the road with a fair degree of comfort and ease. Then suddenly dire tragedy was upon him. The treasures to which he clung were ruthlessly wrung from his hands. The staff upon which he leaned was knocked from under him. The road that seemed so solid beneath his feet became a bog. In his desperate strait he began to wonder if there was not somewhere a hand mighty to help, a treasure that no thief could wrench out of his hands. He began to wonder if there was not a solid roadway that would be beneath his feet

the very Rock of Ages. He may have been made thoughtful by having his heart broken.

3. Or possibly he may have come face to face with a life of such rare spiritual beauty that it made his own seem very paltry and very cheap. Yesterday he was quite smugly content. Yesterday he said with a careless shrug: "I am as good as the average." Then this face came into view and he lost his confident swagger and lapsed into silence. For there was about this life a beauty that he did not possess. There was a peace to which he was a stranger. There was a haunting loveliness that took captive his mind and compelled him to ask for a reason. He was made to think, and in thinking he was driven to the conclusion that God was back of this radiant life, that nobody could account for such rare spiritual loveliness except God himself.

I well remember a turning point in my own life. It was the first time that I ever hungered to know. As a lad I was the despair of the family. At the age of twelve I could not read with any degree of decency. I not only did not know, but what was far worse, I did not care to know. Then one day I was made to think. It came about in this fashion. A beauitful little girl, slightly younger than myself, came to our home for a visit. She was a great reader, but she knew nothing of the country. I was skillful with the horses as well as with the calves. I was an excellent rider, and in her eyes I became a hero overnight.

Really, I have never been quite so great either before or since. But it was too good to last. One morning I went into her room to find her ill. She called to me and said: "I am ill this morning. I want you to read me a story out of one of these books." I felt flattered. No one had ever asked me to read before. They knew better. But my pleasure was short-lived. I could not read her story. But I thought there might be a "getting-out" place. So I said: "I can't read this. I read in the fourth reader." "Get me that," was the reply. I went for the book and, to my sorrow, found it. I then came back a bit like a galley slave at night, scourged to his dungeon. She found a story that she desired to hear, but again I failed. Then, in her surprise she laughed at me a little. But what stung far more, I saw pity in her eyes. She was actually sorry for her one-time hero. Then she said: "You ought to be in the first reader." And you know what I said to her? I said nothing. But what I said to myself was: "Some day I am going to know as much as you."

In one of his books Dr. Sockman has an illuminating chapter on "The Vanishing Sinner." He gives four very keen reasons why this present generation has lost its sense of sin. Somehow I feel like he has left out one supreme reason. The first step, in my opinion, in accounting for the vanishing sinner is the recognition of the fact of the vanishing saint. Wherever there is a sense of God there is always a sense of sin. The purest man must needs put his lips in the dust and cry, "Unclean! Unclean!" when he comes face to face with him. Now this sense of God is a personal experience for some, but for a vast multitude it must come through a Spirit-filled personality. Wherever a truly vital man appears to-day men are still convicted of sin. It was when the dying robber saw himself against the white background of Jesus Christ that he realized his guilt. And in the presence of genuine Christlikeness men are still made to think, they are still made to face the truth about themselves. In the saint they see not only what they are, but they see also what they might be. It may be that this psalmist came upon such a saint one day and became thoughtful and determined to discover his secret.

III

Not only does this poet tell us that he thought, but he tells us that about which he thought. "I thought on my ways." That is hopeful. He could have refused to face the facts about himself. Many of us do. When a glance at our own lives threatens to make us uncomfortable, then we often look about us for some moral pygmy to put us at our ease. We seek out some renegade in the church and think on his ways. We say: "Here is a man who professes to be a Christian. Here is a man who belongs to the Church. But what is the good of it? His life is shoddy. He is only a dishonor to the cause he professes to love. At least I am not a hypocrite. I don't profess to be anything."

And so thinking we fortify ourselves in a course of moral and spiritual weakness and cowardice. Such thinking is fruitful of disaster. This man was wise and brave. He thought of his own case.

Suppose you and I do that. What about our ways? Or to put it more personal still, what about my way?

1. If I may put any confidence in the New Testament, my way is an eternal way. I am on a road that stretches away into the infinite. I may rejoice in this faith with joy unspeakable, or I may be quite indifferent. I may not care for such an endless road. I may wish that my road might terminate at the little ditch that men call the grave. But regardless of my wishes, the road that I travel stretches as far into the eternities as the roadway of God. I shall always be myself, just as you will always be yourself. When all the continents have dropped into the sea, when our little world has ceased to exist, I shall still be journeying on. I am a child of eternity. That ought to make the business of living a high and solemn business. "I have to live with myself, and so I ought to be fit for myself to know."

2. My road has a certain moral direction. That does not mean that I am wholly good, nor does it mean that I am wholly bad. It does mean that the main tendency of my life is either upward or downward. What I am to-night is a question of vast importance. But the most important question about me and the most important question about you is not how far we

have climbed toward the stars, nor how far we have dipped toward the mud. The biggest question is not even what have we become. By far the biggest question is, what are we becoming.

Scientists are fond of telling us how much alike the embryonic man is to the embryonic monkey. One cannot tell the one from the other. But there is a difference, and it is far wider than the spaces between the stars. This difference is in what they are becoming. It is in the vastly divergent directions in which they are traveling. One is traveling out to a life that is essentially of the earth earthy. The other is traveling toward a destiny as deathless as that of God. The baby mocking bird is little more handsome than the baby vulture. But one is facing out toward the life of a scavenger, the other toward green boughs, toward a choir loft in the magnolia trees, toward a concert tour that will lift the soul of the listener and set his heart to dreaming. What is the direction of our lives? That is the big question. If we keep on traveling as we are traveling now, where are we going to park when the sundown comes?

IV

Then the psalmist tells us the outcome of his honest and fearless thinking.

1. When he asked himself as to the direction of his life, when he faced the facts honestly and candidly as to this moral quality of his way, he was forced to the

conclusion that he was traveling in the wrong direction. This does not mean that he recognized himself as a hideous and outrageous sinner. This does not mean that he discovered bloodstains upon his hands and shrieked with Lady Macbeth: "Out, out, damned spot!" But it does mean at least this—that he was forced to say to himself: "Life is not counting for me as it ought to count. I am not realizing the possibilities that I ought to realize. I am not traveling in the direction that I ought to travel. I know that I might use life in a better and braver way than I am using it." And such clear and candid thinking on your part and mine would surely lead many of us to the same conclusion.

2. Then, having reached this true and wise conclusion, he took that next step without which the sanest thinking is futile. Having realized that he was traveling in the wrong direction, he did not content himself by merely wishing that he were going in the right direction. He did not content himself by frankly declaring that he knew himself wrong and that he ought to change his course. When the prodigal came to himself he did more than say, "I wish I were home again," and then lie down among the hogs. He said: "I will arise and go." That was his salvation. This man said: "I am wrong. I will get right. I will turn." That was a most sane thing to do, was it not? In truth, nothing can be more sane than, having recognized that we are going in the wrong direction, to face

about and go in the opposite direction? That is a course of conduct that helps to remake the world, and also sends a thrill through all heaven.

3. The final outcome of this poet's thinking was that it brought him to newness of life. It is this turning that we Christians are accustomed to speak of as conversion. It is what the Bible calls repentance. Whoever so thinks and turns always finds God. This is true without exception. If the worst of men will only dare to turn, he will surely find himself face to face with him who is able to save to the uttermost. God may burst upon the vision of such a one with the suddenness of a flash of lightning, or he may dawn upon him with the slow gentleness of a northern sunrise. But whether suddenly or slowly, the man who so repents will be able to make this entry in his spiritual diary: "I thought on my ways and turned, and turning, found God." May this be a part of the biography of every one!

VII

KEEPING OUR FOOTING

Psalm 73: 2

"But as for me, my feet were almost gone; my steps
had well-nigh slipped."

THIS valiant climber is sharing with us some of the
experiences that he has met along the pilgrim's road.
He has come at last to where he walks with a certain
sureness of step, he feels the road firm and solid beneath his feet because he has learned the secret and
source of strength. But it has not always been so.
As he looks back over his yesterdays he sees one stretch
of road in particular that he found very difficult. In
fact, at this spot he came very near to tripping and
falling headlong. Here he escaped, by the narrowest
margin, losing his footing and slipping into the chasm
that skirted the way, where he might have been seen
and heard no more. He recalls the experience after
these years with mingled terror and gratitude. "I almost slipped. I nearly lost my footing."

This is a bit of the spiritual biography of a man who
struggled and triumphed many centuries ago. Yet his
story is amazingly modern and up-to-date. How thoroughly at home it is in these perplexing days in which
we live! Some of us are saying sadly: "I know ex-

actly what the psalmist is talking about. His experience differs from mine only in this: He managed somehow to keep his footing, but I lost mine altogether.
I went down. I fell prostrate. Since then I have about
quit trying. I have become afraid of that which is
high. Christ's promises are still wonderfully beautiful
and appealing, but for me at least they have not worked
out, and I fear they never will. My feet have slipped,
and I have given up the fight."

Then there are others for whom these words represent a present experience. Though you have not altogether lost your footing, yet you are painfully aware
that you walk in slippery places. You feel that any
moment may bring collapse. You have come out to
God's house this morning, not with any great confidence. You are not at all sure that you will find here
anything to steady you and to enable you to stand
firmly upon your feet. But at any rate you are here,
dimly hoping that such may be the case; that perchance
there may come some word of strength; that there may
be somehow a hand stretched out to help. You are in
sore and desperate need and know not where else to
turn. May God grant that your fainting faith may be
richly rewarded, and that you may go away with a firm
sense of the undergirding of the Everlasting Arms.

I

What was it that came so near to tripping this man
of the long ago? Over what did he stumble? It is

evident that he was greatly bewildered at God's perplexing ordering of things. He could not for the life of him understand how an infinite and holy God could govern the world in the manner in which he felt that the world of his day was being governed. The faith in which he had been reared and to which he clung made his difficulties in this respect only the greater. He had been taught that the good always prosper and that the wicked always go to the wall. That was the faith that was prevalent among all pious Jews at that time. It was old when this psalmist was born and continued long after he had gone to his reward.

For instance, when Job was overwhelmed by one crushing blow after another, there were three men who loved him well enough to undertake to share his sorrow with him. But they assumed at once that, in spite of all appearances to the contrary, Job was being punished for his sin. "It simply cannot be otherwise," they declared emphatically. "Who ever suffered being innocent? Such a thing is simply unthinkable in a God-ordered world. Prosperity is a sure indication of the smile of God; adversity is no less a sure indication of his displeasure and biting indignation."

With this faith also the disciples of Jesus were in hearty agreement. One day, with their Master, they came upon a blind man. This man had been blind from his birth. They asked Jesus: "Who did sin, this man or his parents, that he was born blind?" They could not conceive of any form of calamity, any sorrow, any suffering that was not born directly of the anger and displeasure of God. They believed that without exception the good are prosperous and happy, while the wicked always fail and are always wretched.

There are those who cling to this faith in some measure to this very hour. It is often a very comfortable faith and is therefore one that dies hard. There are those still who believe that God rewards us in the here and now with material and temporal blessings for being good. If he fails to do this, they feel that they have not been treated quite fairly. When they ask for bread, they are rather shocked and disappointed because God refuses to give them a stone. I received a letter only last week telling me of a man who had been a tither all his life, but who, in spite of that fact, had been overtaken by financial disaster. The writer seemed to feel that God should have paid him in dollars and cents for his faithfulness. Now there is no doubt that honesty is in the long run the best policy, and that, all things being equal, a good man stands a better chance at worldly prosperity than a bad man. But even then the good do not always prosper, and when they do, this prosperity is not given in payment for faithful service. We seem to forget that while the devil pays wages, God never does. "The wages of sin is death; but the gift of God is eternal life through Jesus Christ our Lord."

Now it was when this psalmist began to test his faith by the plain facts of experience that he found himself slipping. For when he looked with open eyes upon the world he saw that it simply could not be true. Doubtless there was a neighbor of his that lived not a block away, who despised the worship of the temple and lived in utter disregard of God. This neighbor declared emphatically that he was not in business for his health, that he was in it solely for the money. And there was no denying the fact that he was succeeding amazingly. Everything he touched seemed to turn to gold. Not only so, but both he and his family enjoyed the best of health and to all appearances were finding life exceedingly livable. He was not in trouble like other men; neither was he plagued like other men.

But how about himself? He was trying desperately hard to be a good man. He was diligent in his religious duties. He tithed, he went to the synagogue, he sought earnestly to please God. But what was he getting out of it? Less than nothing. In spite of it all, he was not prosperous. On the contrary, everything he touched seemed to turn to dust and ashes. He declared in bewilderment, not mixed with hot indignation, that he was plagued all day long and that some new chastening came to him every morning. More than once, while in darkness he was sobbing out his perplexities to God, he had been disturbed and half angered by the noise of joyful revelry that had come from the house of his godless and prosperous neighbor.

"It is not fair," he cried hotly into his tear-soaked pillows. "What is the good of my loyalty to my convictions? Surely in vain have I cleansed my heart and washed my hands in innocency. Goodness does not pay, and since goodness does not pay, how can there be a God who cares about our loyalty? How can we be sure that there is a righteous God on the throne when all about us we see the good suffer and the wicked enjoying prosperity? How can any man under such circumstances be sure that 'because right is right to follow right were wisdom in the scorn of consequence?' Is it not possible after all for one to gather grapes of thorns and figs of thistles? Would it not be far wiser for me to follow my neighbor, fling away from God, quit trying to be right, take the cash, and let the credit go?"

And if every one who has at times felt sympathy with the views of this psalmist were to say "Amen," it would shake like an earthquake. There are some of you as indignant over God's amazing ordering of things as was this psalmist. You, too, have tried to be right as God gave you to see the right. But there have been financial losses, sickness, death. So many have been your reverses that at times you doubt the real worth of righteousness. You have chosen to play the game fairly and have lost, while those who played unfairly are winners and are acclaimed for their victory. You had an opportunity for a questionable business adventure, but for conscientious reasons you turned it down. Others without your scruples entered the enterprise and now live in handsome residences on the avenue. "Their eyes stand out with fatness" while you are having a desperate struggle to keep the wolf from the door. Therefore, like this psalmist, you are questioning whether it pays to be true to God or not. You are even questioning whether there is a God who concerns himself about us and our petty affairs. You, too, can say: "My feet are almost gone; my steps are on the point of slipping." Yet it is heartening to know that this psalmist came safely through and ended by finding a firm footing for his feet. So may we, if we are only willing.

II

How did he keep from falling? What was it that steadied him?

He did not find new strength by abandoning all religious faith. He did not find it by flinging away from God altogether. It may be that in your perplexity you feel sorely tempted to do this. It may be that you feel that there is no hope, even in God. But, even assuming that you are right, this is surely true: If there is no hope in him, there is none anywhere. There is certainly nothing to steady us in the thought of a godless world. There is a poem that I have often heard quoted with appreciation, and I am not denying that it has a quantity of desperate courage about it, yet to my mind it is of the very essence of despair.

"Out of the night that covers me,
Black as the pit from pole to pole,

I thank whatever gods may be,
　For my unconquerable soul.

In the fell clutch of circumstance
　I have not winced nor cried aloud.
Under the bludgeonings of chance
　My head is bloody but unbowed.

Beyond this place of wrath and tears
　Looms but the horror of the shade,
And yet the menace of the years
　Finds and shall find me unafraid.

It matters not how straight the gate,
　How charged with punishments the scroll;
I am the master of my fate,
　I am the captain of my soul."

But how pathetically little his captaincy has accomplished! It has only brought him into a night as "black as the pit from pole to pole." It has given him no larger hope for the future than the "horror of the shade." Certainly there is nothing in the renouncing of religious faith to steady our feet.

What then did the psalmist do? The answer to some will seem perfectly childish. He went to church. "I went into the sanctuary of God." O, I know the Church of his day was not perfect. No more is it in our day. Sometimes church services can be very disappointing. Sometimes the preacher contributes but little, and the congregation less. I am afraid that I have preached more than once when the hungry sheep looked up and were not fed. I am afraid that more than once I have darkened counsel with words. Yet it is my conviction that if one turns to God's house with a hungry heart, God will break through a stupid sermon and past the personality of a very commonplace preacher, to the soul that really longs to know him. Just what others got out of this service we are not told. But the psalmist came into possession of certain gripping convictions that steadied him and enabled him to walk in the after days with firmness and assurance.

III

What were these convictions that he glimpsed in the house of the Lord and that he came to hold with clearer vision and with firmer grip through all his later years?

1. He discovered that he had greatly exaggerated the prosperity of the wicked. We constantly tend to think the lot of our neighbor better than our own, especially if we are in trouble. Distance does "lend enchantment to the view." During those dark days of famine in the city of Samaria there is little doubt that the people looked with envy upon the king as he passed by upon the wall. But one day they chanced to see through a rent in his royal garment, and lo, he wore sackcloth within upon his flesh. He had his own secret sorrow. And when this troubled singer looked with clearer and calmer eyes, his hot fever cooled somewhat, for he saw that his wicked neighbor was not so prosperous as he had supposed. It was not that his house was not so fine as he had thought. It was not that his financial

adventures had failed. He saw that though he was still prosperous in things, it was in things only. He had no inner wealth. He was not really joyous and care free, but was "utterly consumed with terrors." Therefore his seeming prosperity was only a hollow sham. It failed utterly to satisfy and thus to make him truly rich.

Then he discovered that the prosperity of the wicked, even though it were ever so satisfying, is fleeting. It simply will not last. The wealth that is ours to-day will belong to another to-morrow. The names that fill the headlines in our papers to-day will have slipped into oblivion to-morrow. "The world passeth away and the lust thereof." "What is needed," an officer asked of Alexander the Great as he looked upon a wonderful pageant, "what is needed to make this perfect?" "It won't last," answered the brilliant young general; "it won't last." The prizes for which we barter our lives slip from our clutching fingers almost as soon as we grasp them. In spite, therefore, of all appearances to the contrary, this world is builded upon a basis of righteousness, and the prosperity of evil is at once superficial and fleeting.

2. He came to realize his own wealth as he came into possession of certain bracing convictions about God. He became sure, first of all, of God's constant presence. "Nevertheless, I am continually with thee." His was not a God afar off who took no interest in the struggles, the sorrows, the heartaches of his child. He

was a God at hand. He was "closer than breathing and nearer than hands and feet." He was at his very side. He was there always. He was near in the sunshine and near in the shadow. He was near when his eyes were sparkling with joy. He was near also when his eyes were blinded by tears. "I have found God," he tells us, "to be a present God. I am with him continually."

Not only was God always present, but he was present to help. "Thou hast holden me by the right hand." The other day I saw a mother going down the street with her little child. For a few steps the little fellow walked alone, but he came to where a crossing was to be made. He then reached up and the mother took his hand and he went forward without fear. "So it has been in my case," says the psalmist. "When the way grew rugged and treacherous and I was in danger of losing my footing, I reached up my hand. And when I did so I did not clutch the thin air. Instead, there was One who seized my hand and held it fast, and who steadied me and gave me guidance."

"Finally I have discovered," says this psalmist, "that God satisfies. If I possess him, I can weather all gales, I can breast all tempests. If I have him, I have enough for time and for eternity." "Whom have I in heaven but thee? And there is none upon earth that I desire beside thee." To have all else but God is to be forever poor and restless and dissatisfied. To have God is to have all. "Lord show us the Father and it is enough."

And because the psalmist has found that God satisfies in the here and now, he believes that he will do so forever. He is firm in his conviction that he will guide him by his counsel and afterwards receive him into glory. That though his flesh and heart fail, as they were sure to do, though the house in which he lived should tumble into ruins, that God would surely be his strength and his portion forever.

In the power of this faith the psalmist was able to keep his feet. In its power he walked bravely forward and so came through his terrible struggle with horror. Such a faith will also steady ourselves. Do we really possess such faith? Do we know in our hearts that there is One infinitely near who is ready to grip our hands in our desperate hours? Do we believe that he abides the same through all the changing years? Are we sure that though friends and health and all else may fail and disappoint, that he never disappoints? Are we fully persuaded that nothing we put into his hand can ever be lost? Such is the conviction of this radiant singer, and those most deeply schooled in the things of God say, "Amen." "Therefore, my beloved brethren, be ye stedfast, unmovable, always abounding in the work of the Lord, forasmuch as ye know that your labor is not in vain in the Lord."

VIII

A RADIANT CERTAINTY

Psalm 56: 9

"This I know, that God is for me." (American Revised Version.)

I

THERE are at present many voices clamoring for our attention. Almost every kind of huckster is crying his wares in the street. Those who have a panacea for all our ills are numerous. But they are little more so than those who despair of any remedy at all. Nor is this confused clamor confined to the affairs of the forum and the market place. It is heard also in the realm of religion. There are many who are seeking with eagerness to tell us what is wrong with the Church. Its faults are glaring, its diseases deadly. "From the sole of the feet to the crown of the head there is no soundness in it," they cry rather zestfully. Meantime there are altogether too few to tell us what is right with God as he is revealed through Jesus Christ our Lord, and as they have found him in their own experiences.

Now, here is a voice to which we can afford to listen. This is true, in the first place, because it is a voice of assurance. Here is a man who speaks with a quiet certainty. There is a ringing conviction in his every accent. He knows what he is talking about. Any man who is an authority in his field, especially if his field is worth while, is worthy of our close and eager attention. Let us tune in on this man and give ourselves a chance to be gripped by his fascinating certainty. How eagerly the crowds gathered about Jesus! What a spell he cast over those with whom he came in contact! Why was this the case? One secret, I am sure, was this: He was a man who knew. "He spake as one having authority."

But not only should we listen to this psalmist because he knows. We should listen with greater attention because of the supreme importance of the knowledge that he has come to possess. "Knowledge is power," is a saying quite hoary with age. There is much of truth in it, too, though it is not universally true. There is a kind of knowledge born of experience that is not power, but weakness. It does not enlighten; it makes one blind. It does not bring life; it rather brings death. We have all come into possession of such knowledge here and there along the way, and we are vastly the poorer for it to this hour. Knowledge of evil never makes for power. The strongest of men was he of whom it is written, "He knew no sin."

In the city of New York a few months ago, a young man, the son of a contractor, ran away with the wife of a multimillionaire. In the eyes of some it was quite a romantic affair. But to those most intimately concerned it proved a tragic disappointment. Ten days later they were found locked in each others arms before a gas jet. On the table was a note written by the woman. It read as follows: "We have been accustomed to laugh, Fred and I, at the moral law as a lot of man-made rules to frighten timid souls into being good. But now we have learned through experience that 'the wages of sin is death'—yea, many times worse than death—hell on earth."

Then there is the type of knowledge that is practically worthless. A man died in one of our larger cities some months ago whose one claim to distinction was that he was good at bridge whist. He was an authority in that realm, but it is hard to persuade ourselves that such knowledge is really worth while. Surely it is not worthy of the devotion of a lifetime. Many of the theological questions about which we grow hot and excited are of little greater importance. How much of our energy has been squandered fighting over questions that are never really settled, in the first place, and that, if they should be settled, would prove of on practical value whatsoever!

Yet there are not a few of us who "major on minors." At present I am thinking of a certain man who enjoys somewhat of a reputation for learning. Nor am I saying that this reputation is not deserved. But I never hear him speak that he does not remind me of one of Edgar Allan Poe's quaint and curious volumes of forgotten lore. He impresses me as knowing more things that are not worth knowing than any man I have ever met. He illustrates how altogether possible it is to be abundant in certain kinds of knowledge and yet share with King James the reputation of being the wisest fool in Christendom.

Then there is a kind of knowledge that is altogether practical and worth while. It falls short, however, in two respects: First, it does not meet our highest needs; second, it is not permanent. "If there be knowledge," said Paul long centuries ago, "it shall vanish away." And how consistently that is being demonstrated as the years come and go! Every reputable scientist will tell you that the theories of to-day are likely to be discredited to-morrow, just as the theories of yesterday are discredited to-day. Nor is he at all ashamed to say this. He knows that the world is going forward. He is therefore ready to sing with Tennyson:

> "Let knowledge grow from more to more,
>   But more of reverence in us dwell;
>   That mind and soul, according well,
> May make one music as before."

But the knowledge possessed by this ancient singer is a knowledge of supreme worth. So priceless is it that, if we miss it, though, if it were possible, we might come to possess all other knowledge, life would still have a pathetic sense of incompleteness. It would still end at last in a tragedy as deep and dark as that woven out of the warp and woof of loneliness and death. If, on the other hand, we come to possess this knowledge, though, if it were possible, we might miss all other knowledge, yet life for us must be victorious in its course and victorious in its consummation. What, then, is this knowledge that is of such supreme and abiding worth? Hear the answer from the lips of the psalmist himself: "This I know, that God is for me."

And the winsome wonder of it is that, though this is the supreme knowledge, it is within reach of every one of us. It has been said wisely that we get most of our knowledge at secondhand. What I know about the north pole I must take on hearsay. I have never been there and never expect to go. What little I know about astronomy I must take from the astronomers. I never intend to map the heavens and thus think God's thoughts after him. In every department of science the vast majority of us must take what the scientists say. But this highest and most worthful of all knowledge is within reach of every one of us. The most handicapped among us may have first-hand knowledge of God.

It is said that one day in London an atheist sought to make sport of an unlettered man who had been converted only a few years before. "Do you know anything about Jesus Christ?" he asked. "Yes, by the grace of God, I do," was the answer. "When was he born?" was the next question. The ignorant saint gave an incorrect answer. "How old was he when he died?" Again the answer was incorrect. Other questions were asked with the same result until the atheist said with a sneer: "See, you do not know so much about Jesus as you thought, do you?" "I know all too little," was his modest answer, "but I know this: Three years ago I was one of the worst drunkards in the East End of London. Three years ago my wife was a broken-hearted woman, and my children were as afraid of me as if I had been a wild beast. To-day I have one of the happiest homes in London, and when I come home at the close of the day my wife and children are glad to see me. Jesus Christ has done this for me. This I know."

II

"This I know, that God is for me." Look at the rich content of this knowledge. How much does the psalmist really know?

1. He knows that God is. Reared doubtless in a pious home, he had believed from childhood in the existence of God. But that was not enough. Then as he grew in knowledge he began to see evidences of God in the world about him. He possibly heard God saying, with Goethe:

> "Before the roaring loom of time I ply
> And weave the garment thou seest me by."

He had seen evidences of God in the silence of the templed hills, in the shimmering song of the brook, in the silver light of the stars. He may have reached the conclusion that earth was crammed with heaven and every common bush aflame with God. He may have found evidences of him everywhere.

But external evidences did not satisfy. They are not enough for you and me. I was brought up in a land of majestic hills and wonderful springs. There were many of these springs that were as abiding as the hills from which they flowed. Amidst the frosts of winter and the drouths of summer they sang with unabated life and gladness. But once I discovered a new spring that I had never seen before. It was in early April after an abundance of rain. The waters of this spring were beautiful and gushing. It looked as if it might flow forever. But when I sought that spring one day in the noontide hush of midsummer there was no water there. There were lovely white pebbles where the spring had once been. There was a little gravel-strewn pathway where it had made its way down the hillside toward the river. Evidences of water were obvious and abundant. But I could not drink evidences. They are a poor substitute when the day is hot and wearying and your tongue is swollen with thirst. This man passed by evidences into a first-hand knowledge of God himself.

2. Not only did he discover that God is real. He discovered that God cares. "This I know, that God is for me." He came to realize through his own personal experience that God loved him individually; that he

singled him out from all those that had lived, and from all those that were then living, and from all those that were yet hidden in the bosom of centuries, to bestow his personal care upon him. What a tremendous and transforming knowledge! Life can never be the same to one who knows in his heart and realizes in the inner deeps of his soul that God loves and cares, not simply for the world, but for him personally.

"But the universe of this psalmist was a small affair," you answer wistfully, "while the bounds of the one in which I live have been pushed back to infinitude." But that does not make God smaller, but greater. That ought to help our faith rather than hinder it. Besides, Jesus has come since that far-off day. As we meet him on the pages of the New Testament we are constantly surprised and thrilled at his amazing love. And this love he gives, not simply to the crowd or to the group, but to the individual. He is incredibly interested and enthusiastic over folks that you and I would hardly have looked at. He gave himself without stint to souls that we would have considered nothing but shoddy. And as he thus squandered his precious energies upon every sort of individual, lepers, prostitutes, and nameless nobodies, he tells us that God is like that. "He that hath seen me hath seen the Father."

3. Finally, the psalmist discovered, not only that God cares, but that he is working on his behalf. He is seeking in every way within his power to bring him to his finest self and to his highest possibilities. This

does not mean that his road was always made soft by a carpet of flowers. God did not coddle him and pamper him. He did not protect him from every rude wind. On the contrary, his road was at times heartbreakingly rough and rugged. He knew what it was to pass sleepless nights. He had an intimate and long acquaintance with tears. But he has become convinced that God is working for his enrichment, not only in spite of all his difficulties, but even through them. His tears are being conserved. They are being kissed into jewels. His losses are being transformed into glorious gains. Thus in the face of disappointment and sorrow he can still sing, "God is for me."

III

What was the effect of this knowledge of God upon the psalmist's everyday life?

1. It gave him a fine high courage. "God is for me," he sings confidently. Therefore, it is only natural that he should go on to say, "What time I am afraid I will trust in thee." His life was beset by many haunting fears. This is true of the most sheltered of us. How many there are with everything in the way of material blessings that heart can wish are yet daily tortured by nagging fears. There are so many foes that can harm us. We are open to attack in so many different quarters. We can suffer in such a multitude of ways. We can suffer in our bodies and in our minds.

We can suffer in the sorrows and heartaches of those whom we love. But this man, because he is so sure of God, has come to where he can look upon life with a fearless heart and quiet eyes.

You remember that dramatic story in the second book of Kings: The servant of the prophet Elisha slips out one morning to discover that the city in which he and his master are stopping is surrounded by a hostile army. Humanly speaking there is no avenue of escape. There is nothing ahead but capture and death. He looks at the strong army with terror and then flees to his master with the despairing cry upon his lips: "Alas, Master, how shall we do?" When the prophet hears the news he begins to pray. No doubt that did not surprise the young man in the least. That he had expected. But when he heard that for which he prayed he was amazed beyond words. For what did Elisha make request? He did not ask for deliverance; he did not ask that God think upon their desperate plight. This was his prayer: "Lord, open his eyes that he may see." And when the eyes of the young man were opened he saw the horses and chariots of fire round about. He came to realize what is abidingly true: "They that be with us are more than they that be against us."

2. This radiant certainty enabled the psalmist to "walk before God in the light of the living." Moffatt translates this "to walk before God in the sunshine of

life." That is, this knowledge enabled the psalmist to live his life in the sunshine. How splendid! There are too many of us that live in the shadows. Our hopes have grown dim. Our expectations have withered. We are not the joyful, radiant saints that we ought to be. What a contrast between ourselves and those whom we meet upon the pages of the New Testament! How wonderfully these dwelt in the sunshine! Some of them were cast into prison, some were stoned, and some were fed to wild beasts. But nothing could rob them of their sunshine. They were somehow taller than the night. No adversity had power to dim their quenchless joy.

> "As some tall cliff that lifts its awful form,
> Swells from the vale and midway leaves the storm,
> Though round its breast the rolling clouds are spread,
> Eternal sunshine settles o'er its head."

Recently I was called back to Memphis to bury a saint who was more than eighty years of age. He had never been famous for either scholarship or ability. Yet his funeral was possibly the largest ever held in that city. Multitudes came because they had been brought under the spell of his radiant life. His last days were marked by bitter losses. His wife slipped away after a fellowship of sixty years. Then a son was killed by a reckless and drunken driver. But through it all there was a stanchness and a fine radiance about this man that simply could not be accounted for except in terms of God. He lived in the sunshine, and eager souls were drawn to him by his radiance. So may we if we are gripped by this bracing faith: "This I know, that God is for me."

IX

THE AGELESS THEME

Psalm 66: 16

"Come and hear, all ye that fear God, and I will declare what he hath done for my soul."

HERE is a man who is determined to get a hearing. He has a story to tell that simply will not keep. He must share it with others. He has an eye more compelling than that of the Ancient Mariner. Not only so, but he seems to throw all timidity to the winds as he hurries to lay eager hands on any chance passer-by that he may constrain him to hear his story. He even reaches those eager hands far across the centuries and puts them upon our listless and preoccupied souls and undertakes to shake us into wakefulness and expectancy. "Listen to my story," he pleads with joyful earnestness. And he bases his appeal, not upon his own eloquence or upon his own wisdom or personal magnetism. He rather bases it upon the abiding worthfulness and fascination of the story he has to tell.

I

What is his theme? What has he to say that he counts with such firm confidence upon winning our interested attention?

He is not claiming our attention that he may discuss the topics of the forum and of the market place. These are matters of passing interest. But they are not of supreme interest to any except those who have the misfortune to be spiritually blind. He is not even asking us to listen to him discuss the best in ancient or modern literature. Not that such a discussion might not be greatly worth while. The importance of books can hardly be overestimated. Paul wrote a letter to a young friend of his years ago. As he wrote a chilling breeze from the Alpine hills fanned the thin hair about his temples and made him shiver. "Dear Timothy," he writes, "Be sure to bring my cloak with you when you come. I left it at Carpus' house in Troas." Then he thought that Timothy might be overloaded, and he added: "If you find you cannot bring all my belongings, leave out the coat and bring my books and parchments. I can afford to have colds and rheumatism, but I simply cannot get on without books." A discussion of books, therefore, might be vastly important and very fascinating, but it is not of supreme importance.

No more is this psalmist seeking to share with us the latest discoveries and guesses of science. Had he done so, his story would have been flung aside and forgotten long centuries ago. For knowledge grows from more to more. Thus it comes to pass that, in the ever-enlarging circle of our horizon, the wisdom of yesterday is in some measure the folly of to-day, and the knowledge of yesterday is the ignorance of to-day.

Science is vastly interesting and vastly important. To some in our modern times it has assumed the proportions of a god. But much that we think we know to-day will be discredited and thrown away to-morrow, for we are marching on. The theme of this poet is therefore more vital and gripping even than the discoveries of science.

What, then, is his theme? He is undertaking to bring us a sure word from God. He is not, mark you, telling his theories or his hopes. He is not even engaging in a theological discussion. He has adventured in the realm of the spiritual and has come into possession of first-hand knowledge of God. It is not of his own deeds that he would speak, but rather of the dealings of God with his own soul. He has a personal gospel. Like the Gospel of Saint Mark, it is good news about God. No wonder, therefore, that we turn eager and wistful faces toward him this morning. No wonder that we lean forward to hear his message that comes to us across the wide spaces of the years. His theme is the most thrilling and abidingly fascinating that these needy hearts of ours can know.

II

What is his story? What has God done for him?

1. God has discovered to him that he is a God who answers prayer. No longer does he speculate as to whether prayer is a form or a force. No longer does he question as to whether there is One, other than

himself, who hears him when he calls, or whether all the values of prayer are purely subjective. He knows that prayer works because it has worked in his own life. He has come to possess an inner strength that he is sure could never have been his except through prayer. He is feeding upon spiritual bread to which he was a stranger till he prayed. His soul is being flooded with a celestial light that he is confident can only shine in through the clear windows of prayer. Yesterday he was overwhelmed by difficulties that seemed destined to work his ruin. He was in the midst of perils of fire and flood. But in answer to his cry God has worked his deliverance and brought him out into a wealthy place. And now he is singing a song of victory that helps to set our hearts to singing as we share with him his bracing faith.

2. God has taught him one of the fundamental secrets of victorious prayer. This psalmist has not succeeded in opening the door to that audience chamber where the soul and God stand face to face only to forget the combination and never to be able to return there again. He now knows the way of approach. He has learned in some measure how to use effectively this mightiest of all forces. For of all the powers that God has entrusted to these hands of ours, there is none that is capable of such mighty and compelling usefulness as prayer. But the tragedy of it is that so few of us know how to use it. Electricity was just as willing to serve Abraham as it is to serve you and me, but he

missed all its benefits because he did not know how to use it. It was just as willing to light the cities and homes of Greece and Rome as those of Europe and America, but they missed its radiance, not because they were prejudiced against it, but through sheer ignorance. And God is just as accessible to you and me as he was to any of the saints of the past. He is just as willing that prayer should be a force in our lives as he was that it should be a force in the lives of Saint Paul or John Wesley or George Müller. But so few of us really know how to pray.

What is the essential of effective prayer that this poet learned? It is obedience. It is a surrendered will. "Whatsoever we ask of him we receive because we keep his commandments and do those things that are pleasing in his sight." Prayer is not tugging at God's skirts like a nagging and spoiled child till we persuade him, against his better judgment, to go our way instead of his. If our way is wrong, if we are outside his will and are willing to remain there, we may pray till the undertaker calls, but we will receive no more answer than did the shrieking priests of Baal. O, the agony of those desperate hours when we are trying to coax God into letting us go our own way! O, the hopeless futility of those prayers that we pray out of unsurrendered and rebellious hearts! It is the effective, fervent prayer of a righteous man, righteous at least in his motives and purposes and in his willingness to be right, that brings results. All other praying is to a sky of brass. "If I regard iniquity in my heart," said this saint, speaking out of the memory of many a futile visit to his closet, "If I regard iniquity in my heart, God will not hear me."

But if there were memories of failures, there were also fresher and gladder memories of victories. From his experience he had learned that when he had ceased to regard iniquity in his heart, when he had been willing at any cost to let God have his way with him, God did hear and answer. He found that he did not have to coax God into his life any more than he had to coax the sunshine into his room. Only lift the blinds and the sunshine bursts in eagerly and gladly, however poor the room may be. Remove the obstruction, or even be willing to have it removed, and God will come in. He is infinitely more eager than ourselves. He even stands at the door and knocks. The psalmist learned this and thus came into possession of the knowledge of how to use the greatest power on earth. And if he learned the secret, so may we.

3. God's supreme lesson to him was a clearer and deeper knowledge of himself. An answer to prayer is always a thrilling experience. It is a great moment in any man's life when God's messenger can say to him what he said to Cornelius: "Thy prayer is heard." But there is something even better than that. That is the new sense of God that comes to him who really prays effectively. God himself is always the best part

of every answered prayer. That is the reason that
prayer is so marvelously transforming.

> "Why, then, should we do ourselves this wrong
> Or others, that we are not always strong?
> That we should ever weak or cheerless be,
> Anxious or troubled,
> When with us is prayer, and joy and peace
> And courage are with Thee?"

III

Here, then, is a man with spiritual springtime bursting upon the morning hills of his heart. No wonder
he is eager to tell his story. Why does he tell it? Why
do we?

1. We do so from sheer necessity. We cannot but
proclaim in some measure what we are. Why is the
rose so red? It is not blushing for our pleasure. That
is its nature. Why does Niagara thunder? It is not
putting on a show to amuse the little handful of tour-
ists that may chance to be present. It cannot help thun-
dering. It has the might of the waters and the shoulders of the heights behind it. Why does Pike's Peak
hood itself in white and wrap a fleecy cape of clouds
about its bony shoulders? It is not tiptoeing for your
benefit and mine. It climbs toward the stars with a
beautiful naturalness. Why does the mocking bird
sing? It sings spontaneously because of what it is.
Even if a staid old apple tree gets springtime into its
heart, it cannot keep it a secret. It must needs proclaim
it to the world by decking itself in garments more win-

some than that of a June bride. And it is for a kindred reason that the psalmist must tell what God has done for his soul. His is the irrepressible speech of a transformed personality.

One day two ex-fishermen, Peter and John by name, were arrested and brought before the highest court of their land. After examination and private conference this wise and learned court reached a decision. "They commanded them not to speak at all nor teach in the name of Jesus." But these men told the court frankly that from sheer necessity they must defy their orders. "We should be most happy to obey," they seem to say, "were it within our power. But obedience is for us a rank impossibility. We cannot but speak the things that we have seen and heard." And what they said was nothing more than sober truth. From the moment that they had been brought into the presence of the court they had been giving their testimony. "Now, when they saw the boldness of Peter and John, . . . they took knowledge of them that they had been with Jesus." There was something about these one-time fishermen that reminded this cultured court of the Christ of God. We declare what God has done for us by what we are.

2. We declare what God has done for us because we are specifically commanded to do so. E. Stanley Jones tells us that Gandhi teaches that no man ought to seek to propagate his religion because he can never be sure that he has found the truth. But the saints and the

seers of the centuries seem, with almost one voice, to contradict him. Certainly he is contradicted by the Bible, and by the New Testament especially. Above all else he is contradicted by Jesus Christ. When he had healed the poor wretch of Gadara his command was, "Go home to thy friends and tell how great things the Lord has done for thee." And when he had risen from the dead he left as his final charge to those who were his this very definite command, "Go and make disciples of all nations." The answer to all who would seek to silence us is that of Peter and John: "We cannot but speak the things that we have seen and heard. . . . We must obey God rather than men." Such may have been a part of the constraint of the psalmist. Such surely is one compelling reason for proclaiming our gospel on the part of those of us who in our hearts call Jesus "Lord."

3. Then we speak from an inner urge that seems to be characteristic of all who, through the centuries, have come into possession of a vital knowledge of God.

This urge belongs to all the great prophets. The golden-tongued Isaiah felt it. One moment we find him with his lips in the dust crying: "Unclean, unclean!" The next, with the consciousness of divine cleansing warming his glad heart, he is crying with a burning eagerness to tell his story: "Here am I; send me." The same is true of Jeremiah. His is a sensitive heart and a tear-wet face. Few, if any, have ever had a ministry that was so difficult and discouraging.

More than once he has longed for a new charge, as many another preacher has done since then. We hear him sighing for a lodging place in the wilderness, that he might leave his people and go from them. On another day, depressed by a sense of the utter futility of his efforts to help, seeing no better returns from his preaching than scorn and persecution, he resolves that he will use a little common sense and never preach again. He makes this resolution in good faith, but finds himself unable to keep it. For the word, he declares, was as a fire shut up in his bones so that to speak was for him an absolute necessity.

This same urge belongs to the saints of the early Church. There were those who had no desire to hear their story. Every agency that the ingenuity of man could devise was used to put them to silence. But they could not be silenced. They cried through the lips of Peter and John: "We cannot but speak." They declared through the lips of Paul: "Necessity is laid upon me." And this was true, not simply of the leaders, but of the rank and file as well. In truth, it is to these nameless nobodies of whom history takes no notice that Christianity owes its rapid spread. It was these that, "going everywhere preaching the Word," set that ancient world on fire. It was these more than the apostles, even, that caused the wilderness and the solitary place to become glad and the desert to rejoice as a rose. That hard pagan world was remade by the dauntless testimony of those who insisted on declaring what God had done for their souls.

And this same holy urge lives in the hearts of God's saints in every walk of life to this day, though we must often feel that it is heartbreakingly rare. "Why do you wish to return to China?" asked Dr. Jowett of a young missionary who had been invalided home. "Because I cannot sleep at night for thinking about them," was his answer. Their hungry hearts, their wealthy possibilities haunted his dreams. He felt that he must tell them his story. And there is John G. Paton pursued through the night by the bloodthirzty people whom he has come to serve. But he does not grow bitter and resentful. He rather cries as he flees for his life: "O, my Tannese, my Tannese, how can I give you up?" And he, too, is in the grip of this same holy passion.

Years ago it was my very great privilege to hear one Mr. Hotchkiss, a Quaker missionary, who had spent fourteen years in the long grass country of Africa. Month after month he toiled at the task of learning the language of those whom he had come to teach. But there was one word for which he had to wait with great patience. That was the word for save. Then one night, after three long years of waiting and working, Mr. Hotchkiss sat by the campfire talking with the chief. In the course of the conversation the latter said: "I was coming through the bush to-day and a man-eating lion got after me and this servant of mine saved me." There was the word at last. At once the missionary sprang to his feet and, putting his hand on the black man's shoulder, asked: "What did you say he did for you?" "Saved me," was the ready reply. "That," answered the missionary, "is what the man Christ Jesus did for you." And the black face lighted up just as millions of other faces have lighted through the years at the hearing of that transforming story. "O, my pale-faced brother," he said brokenly, "that is what you have been trying to tell me for all these weary moons."

Then the speaker added this word of testimony that I shall never forget: "I have been for fourteen years in Africa. I have worked for four years without a companion. I have lived for fourteen months on ants and rhinoceros meat and curded milk. I have had forty-two cases of African fever. But, knowing all that it would mean in loneliness, privation, and suffering, I'd gladly go through it all again to get to see that one black face light up by the camp fire as it did that night." May we possess something of the same holy passion! For it is by our telling our story through word and deed and life that the kingdom of God is to come. And it will come in no other way.

X

MADE FOR MASTERY

Psalm 8: 6

"Thou madest him to have dominion."

THE author of this psalm is evidently writing with his mind and heart saturated with the first chapter of the book of Genesis. He therefore makes three bold and stupendous assertions with regard to man of which our text seems to be the climax. These assertions do not meet with universal acceptance in our scientific age. There are still those who believe them profoundly. There are others who, I fancy, eye them wistfully, only to turn away. There are others still who seem to laugh at them with the cynical laughter of the worldly wise. But whatever may be our attitude toward them, I am very sure that those who accept them possess a sense of the worthfulness of life, and of the dignity of human personality to which all others must forever be strangers.

1. The first daring declaration of this poet is that man is God-made. He believes that we bear upon us the finger marks of the Infinite. He has nothing to say as to the process of man's creation. He is no more interested in processes than is the author of the book

of Genesis. He is not a scientist. He is a poet and
a saint. Therefore he is in no sense concerned with
the how of man's creation, he is only concerned with
who created him. The how is a purely scientific question. It has no religious significance whatsoever. But
the who is of profound importance religiously. And
our psalmist has reached a satisfying answer to this
fundamental question. He believes that man is the
handiwork of God.

2. His second bold assertion is that this God-made
man is a grand creature. He is not a being of no significance and of no importance. He is vastly great and
vastly significant. "Thou hast made him" not "a little
lower than the angels" as the timid translators of the
authorized version say, but "Thou hast made him a
little lower than God." Man is made in God's image.
He is kinfolks with God. He is God's child. He,
therefore, shares somewhat in his Father's nature. He
is like his Father in that he is a personality. By this
we mean that he has power to know, power to love, and
power to choose. The greatest of all the poets was
therefore speaking only sober truth when he sang,
"What a piece of work is man, how noble in reason,
how infinite in faculty; in form and bearing how ex-
press and admirable; in apprehension, how like an
angel; in comprehension how like God." So great is
he that God does for him what he does not do for any
of his planets or solar systems. He is mindful of him

and visits him. He even loves him with an everlasting love.

But, while asserting that man is little lower than God, our author does not mean to affirm that he is wholly divine. The Bible never blinks the fact of man's kinship to the dust. While affirming that he is a son of God, it declares with equal emphasis that he is also a son of Adam. He is, therefore, a strange mixture of the heights and of the depths, of majesty and meanness, of angel and devil, of deity and dust. He has a capacity for wallowing in the mire that is at once horrible and amazing. He has also a capacity for fellowship with God and for positive likeness to God that is even more amazing. He is, therefore, a bewildering complexity, neither wholly good nor wholly bad. But this fact does not in any sense discount his essential greatness. In spite of his incredible contradictions, the psalmist regards him as a marvelous creature, close akin to God.

3. The final assertion of this poet-saint is that this great creature is made for a high and worthy destiny. He is not here by mere chance. He is not here as the plaything of his environment. He is not here to be the bondslave of his fellows. Nor is he here to be the slave of blind force. He is here in accordance with the plan of God. His Creator has a purpose for him, and that purpose is dominion. He is made for mastery. He is destined for kingship. His brow is meant for crowning. He is to be master over all the lower orders

of life. He is to be master of himself. He is even
to have dominion over his fellows in so far as that
dominion is the result of mutual self-subjection out of
reverence to Christ.

II

We are aware, of course, that there are many who do
not accept the psalmist's conception of man's lofty
place in the scheme of things. There are varied shades
of opinion that darken into the blackness of flat con-
tradiction. It is rather the order of our day to belittle
man rather than to magnify him, to cater to his conceit
and at the same time rob him of that "self-reverence,
self-knowledge, self-control that alone lead life to sov-
ereign power."

1. He is belittled by being robbed of his high origin.
For many he is no longer the child of an infinitely
loving Father who has made him to have dominion.
He is rather "the product of blind forces that had no
prevision of what they were creating." He is, therefore, without the slightest significance to those forces
that brought him into being. To such blind powers
a Saint Paul can mean no more than an angleworm,
and a Jesus of Nazareth than a handful of slime.

2. He is also belittled by his environment. The universe of which he is a part has become so great that
he has been made to seem immeasurably small. Our
psalmist felt something of this in his day. "When I
consider thy heavens, the work of thy fingers; the

moon and the stars, which thou hast ordained; what is man, that thou art mindful of him?" One of our keenest Christian writers said recently that it is hard to believe that a God who holds the milky way in his hand takes note of the doings of individual men. Many seem to take with crass literalness Mark Twain's humorous story of the man who went to heaven from California. Arrived at the pearly gates, this gentleman is asked from whence he comes. He tells them proudly, "From California." But nobody knows where California is. "It is in the United States," declares the new arrival with amazement. But nobody knews where the United States it. "It is in North America," he exclaims. But nobody knows where North America is. "It is a part of the earth," he continues with growing indignation. But nobody knows where the earth is. At last some of the wise scholars, after a long search, find that the earth is a little forgotten speck, flung out into space, that was once known as "The Wart." Naturally, if man's world is so insignificant, he himself would seem infinitely more so. Thus has he been dwarfed by his environment.

3. Finally, man is belittled by his loss of freedom. According to certain of our biologists and psychologists, man is not made for mastery, he is rather made to be a slave of his biological inheritance or the plaything of outward stimuli. One has called this modern loss of freedom "the second fall of man," in contrast

to his fall when his freedom was denied by the stern doctrine of Calvinism. But this second fall is infinitely the more disastrous. Hideous and repellent, in many respects, as was the Calvinistic creed, it was undeniably man-making. It gave to life for those who accepted it a profound significance. "The meanest of them," says Macaulay, speaking of the Puritans who were the product of Calvinism, "the meanest of them was a being to whom a mysterious and terrible importance belonged, upon whose slightest action the powers of light and darkness looked with anxious interest." "It was an iron creed," writes another, "but it made iron men." But faith in this modern loss of freedom is in no sense man-making. It reduces man to a mere machine. It makes it easy to see in him nothing bigger or better than "a parasite on the epidermis of a midge planet, a monkey that chatters to himself of kinship with the archangels while he filthily digs for groundnuts."

III

How refreshing to turn from this nightmare of unbelief to the sane and ennobling faith of this psalmist!

1. I accept his view of man because such a view enlists my desire. It gives me the will to believe. While I was a student at Harvard a friend told me this story which I dare say is not true, but still it is to the point. "I was going," said he, "from Boston to New York. At New Haven a friend joined me, a

student at Yale, who was also headed for New York. When we were seated I noticed his railroad ticket protruding from his pocket, so I slipped it out and into my own. A moment later he missed it, told me of his loss, and we searched for it frantically. At last he told me that he had no money for his fare. I answered that I, too, was penniless. Then I offered a suggestion. I told him to get under the seat as best he could and that I would spread my overcoat over him so that the conductor could not see him. He reluctantly consented. But he had not been long in his humiliating and uncomfortable position when the conductor came by. I gave him two tickets. 'Where is the other passenger?' he asked. 'He is under the seat,' I answered. 'He just prefers to ride that way.'" Even so I prefer to travel life upheld by the bracing faith of the psalmist.

2. Then I side with our poet because his position appeals to my intelligence. This is not the case because faith has no difficulties. It has, but as I see it, they are as mole hills to mountains in comparison with the difficulties of unbelief. It may be hard to believe that man is God-made, but it is still harder to believe that he is mud-made or chance-made. It may be difficult to accept his significance in a universe that stretches into infinity, while we are reminded that the average man is so small that all the chemical elements that enter into his making would be worth in the current market only ninety-eight cents. But it is harder still to doubt his significance when we realize that, with

all his smallness, he can contemplate his universe, map
its solar system, and measure its planets; that, more
amazing still, he can dream and hope and love, while
the stars with all their incredible bulk can do none of
these things. It may be difficult to believe that he is
a free personality, but it is more difficult still to believe
that he is mere machine. Machines do not reproduce
themselves. When my car wears out it does not leave
a better in its place. Besides, I am conscious of the
fact that "I am I, with power on mine own act and on
the world."

3. I take the poet's view because of the evidence of
its truth that I see in the world about me. That man
is a great creature, made for mastery, is evidenced by
the fact that his mastery is even now in process of
realization. He is already master over the lower orders
of life. All the beasts of the field acknowledge his
kingship. He is gaining increasing mastery over nature. Deadly diseases that once decimated whole popu-
lations have been put out of commission. He has made
the lightning his servant and the ether waves his mes-
sengers. He has learned to outswim the fish and to
outfly the eagle. Years ago a man wrote an incredbile
story called *Around the World in Eighty Days.* Recently two daring aviators flew around the world in
little more than one-tenth of that time. We also dare
to believe that man has made progress in the realm
of the moral and spiritual. This is a far better world
than it used to be. There are wrongs that once were

regarded as inevitable that are now intolerable, thanks to countless saints who yesterday and to-day have salted the earth.

IV

But while recognizing the fact that progress has been made, we cannot fail to see that we are still very far from realizing the mastery that is God's dream for us. There remains yet very much land to be possessed. With the author of the letter to the Hebrews we can say, "We see not yet all things put under him." So busy have we been in competing and fighting in our efforts to gain dominion over each other that we have fallen far short, even in the realm of the material, of the mastery that is a part of God's purpose for us. This is evidenced by the fact that, in a world that is amply able to supply the physical needs of every man, woman, and child, multitudes yet live under conditions that dwarf the body, stultify the mind, and starve the soul.

Then how far we fall short of dominion in the realm of the spirit! How few possess that inner mastery that enables them to say with their Lord, "I have overcome the world." We are still the slaves of things, of our own ambitions and appetites, of our lusts and passions. We are the slaves of sin, for "he that committeth sin is the bondslave of sin." And this is the most galling of bondages. It is the only bondage that kills. "Stone walls do not a prison make, nor iron bars a cage."

Many of the saints were never more free than when they were in prison cells.

> "He that has light, within his own clear breast,
>   May sit i' th' centre, and enjoy bright day;
> But he that hides a dark soul and foul thoughts,
> Benighted walks under the mid-day sun;
> Himself is his own dungeon."

Now, it is just this inner freedom and mastery that is God's plan for us. It is also this that Jesus is constantly offering. When he preached his first sermon in his own home church, this was a part of his text, "The Spirit of the Lord is upon me, because he hath anointed me, . . . to set at liberty them that are bruised." He was constantly declaring confidently: "If the Son shall make you free, ye shall be free indeed." And this sense of freedom, of inner dominion, was the joyous experience of all those who came to know him. "He hath loosed us from our sins and made us kings," shouts John. "And this same spiritual kingship is for you," he declares confidently, "for whatsoever is born of God overcometh the world." It was their sense of inner mastery and their passion to share it with others that sent them to set the world on fire.

> "Oft when the spell is on me to deliver,
>   Melts the illusion and the truth lies bare,
> Desert or throng, city or the river
>   Fades into lucid paradise of air
> Only like souls I see, the folk thereunder
>   Slaves who should conquer, bond who should be kings

Hearing their one hope with an empty wonder
  Sadly content with the show of things.
Then with a burst the intolerable craving
  Shivers through me like a trumpet call,
O to save them, to perish for their saving,
  Die for their life, be offered for them all."

How, then, shall we win this mastery that is God's purpose for us? We are not going to win by force. The supreme tragedies of history have been born of man's effort to gain dominion through force. Such dominion has not only been expensive in human blood, but it has always been superficial and fleeting. We are not going to win through any form of self-seeking. The one essential of real mastery is self-mastery, and that only comes through self-surrender. This was the experience of Paul. He found his higher self at war with his lower self. This better self was constantly being taken captive and brought under subjection. At last, with the desperate cry, "O wretched man that I am! Who shall deliver me," upon his lips, he threw himself in utter surrender into the arms of his Lord. It was then and then only that he found victory. He was therefore speaking out of his own experience when he wrote later, "The fruit of the Spirit is love, joy, peace, . . . self-control."

It is through this self-mastery that we win the only mastery over our fellows that is legitimate and abiding. This was the secret of the spell that Livingstone cast over the little handful of followers that shared with

him the perils and pains of darkest Africa. Why, when
he died, did they carry his body, in spite of savage
beasts and more savage men, through those hundreds
of miles of jungle to give it into the keeping of his
friends from far-off England? It was not because he
had conquered them by force, but because he had taken
captive their hearts through the love of a surrendered
life. This is the kind of dominion that Jesus is seeking. It is dominion over our hearts. He knows that
all other mastery is futile. Napoleon came to realize
that he and other conquerors had established their
kingdoms by force only to see them fall to pieces, while
Jesus had established his through love to see it abide
and to have millions through all the centuries that
would gladly die for him.

This is the mastery that is necessary for the stabiliz-
ing and beautifying of our home life. The modern
home is passing through sore straits. It is a bit like
the house of which the Master spoke that was founded
upon the sand. Many a rude wind is to-day beating
against it, and often tragically it is falling into ruins.
One tempest that cannot fail to work disaster is for
husband and wife each to determine at any cost to be
the head of the home. Yet Maggie, in *Bringing Up
Father*, seems to be the ideal of all too many of both
sexes. Hers is the dominion of force. It is the mastery of the rolling pin. But how futile it is! No sooner
is her back turned than Jiggs is gone again to his old
crowd and to his corned beef and cabbage.

But here is a type of mastery that is real and abiding. Some years ago a magnificent looking man with a frail slip of a woman on his arm, passed along the deck of a transatlantic steamer. She was thin and wasted and was very evidently a physical wreck. As they passed by in their stroll a vigorous woman said softly to her neighbor: "What a pity it is for a splendid man like that to be the slave of such a frail, invalid wife." The husband overheard the remark and when he had taken his wife to her stateroom came back and sat down beside the woman who had made it, and said: "I could not help hearing what you said a moment ago about my being a slave to my wife. I just came to tell you that you used the right word."

"A few years ago," he continued, "my business failed through the rascality of a partner that I held in highest confidence. He made it appear that his dishonesty was mine, and everybody thought me guilty except one. That was my wife. My health broke under the strain. But she stood by me, fought for me, compelled me to believe in myself, and at last I got on my feet again. But the drain upon her energies had been too great. Her health was completely wrecked. She gave herself in order to save me. And now, I repeat, you used the right word. I am her slave, and my fondest wish for you is this, that some day you may be able to command as willing a slave."

This home was saved through the mutual self-giving of husband and wife. The world is to be saved on the same principle.   When men are willing to be in subjection one to another out of reverence to Christ, then the kingdom of God will have come and man will have entered into possession of that mastery which is God's dream for him.

XI

MY TONGUE

Psalm 39: 1

"I will take heed to my ways, that I sin not with my tongue."

HERE is a man who has resolved to control his tongue. Most of us know perfectly well how to sympathize with him in his great decision. So much is this the case that we feel that we might even be able to trace with considerable accuracy some of the steps by which he reached his high resolve. Probably one evening he had gone for a visit to the house of a friend. There were other guests present, and they conversed long and freely. Their conversation, unfortunately, turned largely upon personalities. He himself wielded the sword of his tongue skillfully and merrily. He was decidedly interesting. Many times his sallies of wit were greeted by gales of laughter. As he took his way home he was at first rather proud of himself. He felt as if he had been the toast of the evening.

But when he had reached home and was preparing for some much-needed rest, just as he was dropping off to sleep a witty and cutting remark he had made about an absent friend slipped into his mind. He remembered the laughter that had greeted that bright remark. But in spite of the success of his well-aimed shaft, he now felt his face grow hot as he thought of it. His bed somehow became a thing of stone. His pillows were stuffed with nettles. "What a fool I was," he said to himself bitterly; "what a cruel, ungrateful fool to allow myself to talk like that! Henceforth I will take heed to my ways that I sin not with my tongue."

But this poet doubtless soon found that he had undertaken a difficult task in setting himself to control his tongue. Mastering the tongue is no easy matter. If we have not found that out, it is probably because we have never seriously undertaken the conquest. James, in his classic passage on the tongue, declares that while man has succeeded in taming all kinds of monsters, both on land and sea, he has not yet made much headway with the tongue. "It is a restless evil," he declares truly. Just as you have seen a wild beast pace back and forth in its cage, ready to snap at any hand that is reached toward it, ready to dash out the door and back to its old life of savagery at the slightest opportunity, so it is with these restless tongues of ours. They, therefore, need constant guarding. They are harder to subdue, declares the practical James, than the creatures of the jungle.

But in spite of the difficulty of the task, this psalmist resolutely undertook it. And we ought to see with clearer eyes than he the absolute necessity of our doing the same. If James is right, there is simply no being vitally religious while we let our tongues run loose. If we claim to be Christian and at the same time talk recklessly, he tells us that our Christianity is a sheer futility. Jesus Christ and an unbridled tongue cannot live in fellowship. "If any man among you seem to be religious, and bridleth not his tongue, this man's religion is vain." But, if he does bridle his tongue, then he has at least one mark of Christian perfection. According to James, he has measured up to one big test of moral and spiritual maturity. "If any man offend not in word, the same is a perfect man, and able also to bridle the whole body."

I

What are some of the sins of the tongue? We might mention many. There is the foolish habit of profane swearing. There is the course and filthy jest. Whoever engages in unclean talk is unclean at heart, though such a one may be outwardly as chaste as Diana. There is the sin of insincerity in speech, the lies that we tell, white or gray or black. Then there are the harsh words that we utter to one another in our anger. These often wound far more deeply than blows. As a teacher of boys I have found by actual experience that I could inflict corporal punishment upon a boy and retain his warm friendship. In fact, there were times when our friendship even seemed deepened by the ordeal. But friendship is seldom possible where harsh and abusive language is used. Love and friendship cannot live long in the atmosphere of a perpetual war whoop.

But the particular sin that we wish to consider now is the sin of the faultfinder, the gossip, the talebearer. This is a type of sin that is repeatedly rebuked in the Bible. One old law says, "Thou shalt not go up and down as a talebearer among thy people." The author of the fifteenth Psalm, in enumerating those who are going to be able to stand before God, puts among the first the man that "backbiteth not with his tongue." Paul, according to Moffatt, writes to the Romans (14: 13): "So let us leave off criticizing one another." And Jesus says: "Judge not, that ye be not judged. For with what judgment ye judge, ye shall be judged; and with what measure ye mete, it shall be measured to you again."

Now this kind of sinning with our tongues is exceedingly prevalent. We find it practiced by those fiction writers who, seeing and reporting only the worst, allow themselves to degenerate into creatures little better than literary scavengers. We meet it among those writers of biography who are fond of debunking the heroes of the past by showing us that they are not heroic at all, but the commonest of common clay. We find it in certain newspapers that glorify crime, that paint the bootlegger as a hero and a martyr if he is killed while violating the law, and the enforcement officer as a fool if he is killed in line of duty. We

also find it in those papers of the jingo type that seek to
create friction between nation and nation. We find it
in our social contacts where we so often amuse ourselves by playing loose with the good names of each
other.

II

What harm does the man do who thus sins with his
tongue?

1. The faultfinder injures himself. "The tongue,"
says Jesus, "defiles the whole body." That is profoundly true. The mud slinger cannot engage in his
favorite pastime without getting some of the mud that
he slings both upon his hands and upon his heart.
How often we have come away from such an experience with a sense of defilement! Yet that was not
our intention at all. We were vainly hoping that by
slinging mud upon others we might enhance some one's
estimate of our own cleanliness. We were foolish
enough to believe that we could build ourselves up by
tearing another down. We were blind enough to fancy
that by putting a stick of dynamite under the house of
our neighbor we could strengthen the foundations of
our own. But this is never the case. In our effort to
injure others we may succeed, but we always inflict
the depeer injury upon ourselves.

It is easy to see why this is the case. The faultfinder seeks for the worst instead of the best. Seeking
for the worst, he finds it. Finding it, he so fixes his

gaze upon it that he misses the good altogether. Pick out the best man you know and set yourself to find fault with him, and you will succeed. Begin to publish his faults and you will come to distrust him. Keep it up and your district will become contempt. Persist still further and your contempt will harden into hate. Experience has doubtless demonstrated to some of us that it is possible to criticize another who has done us no wrong at all till we come to believe ourselves really injured and till we come further positively to hate the one that we have falsely persuaded ourselves has injured us. Faultfinding, therefore, is harmful because it is a sin against love.

Then it works vast ill in that it ministers to our pride and self-satisfaction. As a rule, the more we find fault with others, the less fault we have to find with ourselves. The man who was keen enough to see a mote in his brother's eye was blissfully unconscious that he had a whole tree trunk in his own. The Pharisee who classed all other men as extortioners, unjust, and adulterers, had no fault to find with himself. In fact, he regarded himself as a paragon of piety. The supreme devil of literature, I take it, is Iago. So low does he sink that he comes to take pride in that which is the very badge of his devilishness. "I am nothing if not critical," he says with a swagger. How deadly, therefore, is that habit that kills our humility and our love and brings us to take a supreme pride in what should be our supreme shame.

2. Then the faultfinder hurts the man he criticizes. Oftentimes he wounds him to the very heart. Some of the bitterest suffering that this world has known has been inflicted by the unbridled tongue. The writer of the sixty-fourth Psalm pictures the reckless talker as shooting arrows at his victim. Those arrows are not made of stone or steel. They are made of words, sharp, bitter, poisonous words. Therefore they do not kill in a moment. Maybe they never kill at all. But they rankle and torture and sometimes leave old wounds that never heal. There is no estimating the exquisite pain that fine, sensitive souls have suffered through wounds inflicted by the tongue.

There are those brave and strong enough to disregard in large measure the harsh criticisms directed against them. Yet even these do not always escape the faultfinder unscathed. If such are not hurt in their feelings, they are hurt in their reputations. And the one who injures my reputation also injures my usefulness. For the measure of my power to help is at least in part the measure of the confidence that I can command. Yet I have known parents to openly criticize their minister in the presence of their children, and then be surprised and pained that he whose reputation they had destroyed was not able to win their children. But the failure of that minister was not due to himself alone. His chance of success had been killed by those seeking his help.

Not only is faultfinding an attack upon the reputation and usefulness of the victim, but it is an attack upon his character as well. I know that nothing said against us can destroy our characters. But it can do this: It can take from us one of the greatest safeguards of character. What greater help is there toward the living of a right life than the confidence of one's fellows? That old saying, "Give a dog a bad name and he will justify it," has lived because there is so much truth in it. It is hard for one to fall who is undergirded by a firm and steadfast confidence. But how easy it is if everybody expects that one to do so! Therefore, the faultfinder makes war upon the feelings, the reputation, and the character of his victim.

> "Who steals my purse steals trash; 'tis something, nothing;
> 'Twas mine, 'tis his, and has been slave to thousands;
> But he that filches from me my good name
> Robs me of that which not enriches him
> And makes me poor indeed."

3. Then the faultfinder hurts his hearer. Of course this hearer is too often willing to be hurt. Those to whom we carry tales, to whom we gossip in an evil way, usually welcome such liberties. We cannot broadcast our criticisms unless some one tunes in on us. The listener therefore becomes a sharer in the crime of the speaker. If the critic is guilty of stealing a reputation, then the listener is guilty of receiving stolen goods. Both, therefore, meet the same condemnation. Also the injuries that the faultfinder inflicts upon himself are shared by the receiver of his confidences.

4. Finally, faultfinding is a sin against society. There is no telling the evil that one lie can accomplish. "The tongue is a fire," says James. Having started a blaze, there is no telling where the blaze will stop. The beauties of the great forests of the Northwest lift the heart and set the soul to dreaming. But I have seen these great forests become charred and blackened ruins because perchance some smoker had been careless in the handling of a match. And ruins more ugly and tragic than these are often left in the wake of the careless wielder of the tongue. Society is founded upon confidence. Destroy confidence and the whole social fabric falls to pieces. The faultfinder is a destroyer of confidence and is therefore an enemy both to the individual and to the group.

III

No wonder, then, that this wise psalmist highly resolved that he would no longer sin with his tongue. Surely we, too, are ready to join him in his high resolve. But having resolved, how may we hope to succeed? To help us in this direction let me offer the following suggestions:

1. Before we find fault let us realize how unfair it is for us to do so unless we have all the facts in hand. Let us realize further how impossible it is for us to know all the facts. We may live with each other for half a century and then know each other only superficially. It is utterly impossible for any human being

to be absolutely sure that he is rightly judging his brother. How often we are forced to say, "I should not have been so harsh and unkind if I had only understood." But we never know fully. Therefore Jesus says, "Judge not." That is a prerogative that belongs to God and to God only. Let us beware of usurping the throne of the Almighty. "Who art thou that judgest another man's servant?"

2. Then it might help us to realize that our judgments, however carelessly and hastily made, often have a terrible finality. We always make them without a full knowledge of the facts. Many times we find, after rendering our decision, that we were altogether wrong. Yet having uttered our hasty judgments, we cannot fully recall them, however eager we may be to do so.

"Boys flying kites haul in their white-winged birds,
But you cannot do that way when you are flying words."

We may be brave enough and honest enough to try to correct our false report, but there are always those who heard the lie that will never hear the correction. Years later that old forgotten lie may arise in a vague question with regard to its victim: "Did I not hear something bad about him once?" And to be questioned is often to be condemned.

One day my brother and I kindled a fire in an old stump that stood in the center of a field that was rank with dry grass. Father did not want the grass burned. Therefore we were a bit careful. But in spite of our

care a spark flew out and started a little blaze that
began to spread rapidly. We at once saw the danger.
Therefore we each grabbed a branch of a tree and
began to fight the fire vigorously. We soon succeeded
in extinguishing the blaze that was immediately in
front of us. But we looked up a moment later to discover that by our very efforts to put out the fire, we
had scattered it in a dozen different directions. We
were sorry and tried hard to correct our blunder, but
the grass was burned none the less, and the fences too.
Such is often the case with the fires that we kindle with
our tongues. In our very effort to extinguish them we
only spread them.

3. Then it might be well for us to face the facts as
to what lies behind our faultfinding. Why do we thus
let our tongues run loose? Does it come of anything
big or brotherly in us? What is the source of this fire
called the tongue? Here again James comes to our
assistance. He says that the tongue of the faultfinder
is set on fire of hell. That is an ugly truth, but we
need to face it. Harsh and unkind criticisms are not
born of heaven; they are born of hell. They are not
the outcome of love, they are the outcome of hate.

Who is Satan anyway? He is the slanderer. He
is the traducer of the brethren. "Hast thou considered
my servant Job, that there is none like him in the earth,
a perfect and an upright man, one that feareth God,
and escheweth evil?" What is Satan's answer to this
question? He fairly shakes with laughter. He turns

to the Almighty and says: "I am surprised at you. It is amazing how easily you are duped. I know Job is outwardly decent, but it is because you are paying him a big salary. You are protecting him and feeding him bonbons. Does Job serve God for naught?" The devil explains away all goodness. That is what makes him such a success as a devil. Just in proportion as we pursue his course, we become kinfolks with him.

4. But our supreme asset in the subduing of our tongues is pointed out by the author of the hundred and forty-first Psalm. He had evidently had trouble with his tongue. He had, possibly, spent more than one sleepless night brooding over the havoc it had wrought. At last, despairing of ever gaining the victory in his own strength, he turned to God and poured out this wise prayer: "Set a watch, O Lord, before my mouth; keep the door of my lips." And we may be sure that the God who answers prayer was not deaf to the appeal of this tongue-tortured man. No more will he be deaf to your appeal and mine. In our conflict with our tongues he can make us more than conquerors.

How will he do it? He will not do it by putting a padlock upon our mouths, but by taking captive our hearts. He will not compel us to silence, but cause us to speak according to the law of love. This is the great need. For the tongue, of course, is not an evil in itself. It may be an unmeasured good. It all depends upon how we use it. If it can sting like an

adder, it can also heal like a mother's kiss. If it can
steal our courage and leave us limp, it can also breathe
battle into us and send us out to fight where the victory
is to the brave. If love rules, there is nothing to fear.
"Love worketh no ill to his neighbor," not even the
ill of an unkind word. Let us therefore join with this
struggling psalmist in his victorious prayer: "Set a
watch, O Lord, before my mouth; keep the door of
my lips."

XII

THE TRANSIENCY OF TEARS

Psalm 30: 5

"Weeping may endure for a night, but joy cometh in the morning."

WHAT a gem of a text! Of course there are many who do not believe it, who feel that it is beautiful poetry and nothing more. There may be those who have found life especially hard, who will fling away from it indignantly, declaring that it simply is not true, that their tragic experiences have demonstrated its utter falsity. But its truth or falsity aside for the moment, surely it is a faith that is well worth possessing. To those who flatly declare that they cannot believe it I think our poet would say what the artist, Turner, said to a woman who could see no fidelity in his picture of the sunset. "Why, Mr. Turner," she said, "I never saw a sunset like that." "Aye, Madam," was the answer, "but don't you wish you could?" "O, poet of the sunny face," you may cry wistfully or petulantly, "I cannot share your optimistic faith." "Aye," he answers, "but don't you wish you could?"

What is the faith of this psalmist? He is daring to tell us that in this world of change and decay, in this world where our hearts are so often broken and our faces so often wet with tears, that joy may be a more abiding guest than sorrow. He does not promise exemption from sorrow. He makes no claim to the discovery of an ideal world. But what he does say is that while weeping may come in as a wayfarer and spend the night, that the unwelcome guest need not abide, that he need not establish himself upon our shoulders like an old-man-of-the-sea. He may remain for the night, but he cannot abide the dawning of the day. Tears may come, but they will be transient. With the rising of the sun they will vanish like the dew or be kissed into jewels by its splendor. "Weeping may endure for a night, but joy cometh in the morning."

What a beautiful reading of things, and how refreshingly unique! It is just the opposite of the commonly accepted view. Are we not constantly reminding ourselves of the transiency of our joys? How often, for instance, we look upon the innocent and care-free play of children with a mingling of envy and pity. How joyful they are, and how soon they must leave it all behind, pass out of their Eden of morning gladness into a harsh and rugged world where the stones will bruise their feet and where the thorns will pierce not their bodies only, but their hearts as well. How fleeting is the springtime of life! And the springtime of the heart is often more fleeting still. Byron found it so:

" 'Tis not on youth's smooth cheek alone
  The blush that fades so fast,
But the tender bloom of heart is gone
  Ere youth itself is past.

O, could I feel as once I felt
  And be what I have been
And weep as I could once have wept
  O'er many a vanished scene.

As springs in deserts found seem sweet
  All brackish though they be,
So midst the withered waste of life
  Those tears would flow to me."

Then there is the joy of courtship between a man
and a maiden, the thrill of a growing love, the romance
of marriage, the gladsome glamor of the honeymoon,
the sweet climax of the making of a home. But we
are told that these joys are also fleeting. Too often
the romance does not outlast the honeymoon. The
radiance soon dies and wedded life sinks down into the
dull, drab commonplace. The other day we were to
have a wedding at the church of which I am pastor.
As I was going in to perform the ceremony I noticed
the car in which the bride and groom were to go to the
station to begin their honeymoon. Somebody had dec-
orated it with a flaring placard which pictured a man
and a woman glaring angrily and disgustedly at each
other. Under the picture were these words: "When
you get what you want, you don't want it." Of course
it was only a joke, but it is too often the tragic truth

to be amusing.   And even where love lives and our dreams come true, sorrow soon calls.   How lovely was the home of your childhood, but to-day that home is only a memory.   There is no road that leads to it, for it is a part of a buried yesterday.

This note of the transciency of our joys is one that sobs its way through much of our literature.   Every one knows that—

> "Pleasures are like poppies spread,
>   You seize the flower, the bloom is shed;
>   Or, like the snowfall in the river,
>   A moment white, then melts forever."

Again we say urgently:

> "Gather ye rosebuds while ye may,
>   Old Time is still a-flying,
>   And this same flower that smiles to-day
>   To-morrow will be dying."

Or we sing plaintively:

> "Sweet day, so cool, so cal.n, so bright,
>   The bridal of the earth and sky;
>   The dew shall weep thy fall to-night;
>   For thou must die."

And old Omar with his mug of wine at his lips, seizes us almost rudely by the shoulders and shakes us frantically, urging us to drink and enjoy our fleeting moment of laughter while we may.

> "A momentary taste of happiness amid the waste,
>   Then the nothing we set out from, O make haste."

Shakespeare also speaks to the same purpose, showing us a man on the point of arriving only to be quickly overtaken by disaster. "And when he thinks, good easy man, full sure his honors are a-ripening, then comes a frost, a killing frost." And so they go on endlessly with their songs of the transiency of joy. But here is a glad voice raised to tell us that it is weeping that is soon gone. It may tarry for a night, but joy will surely come with the morning.

II

How did our poet come by this conviction?

It is heartening to realize that his faith is not born of a stubborn refusal to face the ugly facts of life. He does not believe that weeping will abide only for a night because he has shut his eyes to the grim tragedies that are the fountain source of our tears. How fruitful in tears, for instance, is the horrid fact of sin. But this poet does not deny the reality of sin. No more does he deny the reality of pain. Nor does he deny that final calamity called death. He faces all the terrifying foes that encompass us and still clings to his buoyant faith.

Then we may be further heartened by the fact that this bracing text is not the easy optimism of one who has lived on the sunny side of the street and has had everything come to him right side up. There is something positively provoking in the cocksure preaching of one who has never put the efficacy of his gospel to the test. This was what made old battle-scarred Carlyle rage at times against the complacent optimism of Emerson. He felt that this man whose voyage had been so largely over smooth seas had no right to speak with such assurance to those who had encountered little else than seas that had been whipped into rage by fierce tempests. But this poet is speaking out of his own experience. That is the glory of these psalms. They were lived before they were written. When, therefore, this singer tells us that, though weeping may tarry for a night, joy will come with the morning, he is telling us a truth to which he has come by the painful path of experience. He is bringing us a conviction that, at great cost, he has hammered out upon the anvil of his own soul.

He even traces for us the road along which he traveled to his sunny faith. For years life dealt most kindly and gently with him. Sickness and sorrow came to others, but not to him. The hearse drew up in front of other homes, but not in front of his. He knew that suffering and tears were a part of the human lot, but he did not realize it. Reports of the tragedies that were taking place day by day in the lives of men and women all about him seemed somehow strangely remote. He tried after a fashion to enter into sympathy, but could not. The stories of their sorrows seemed to come to him from a distant world. So long did his prosperity continue that it intoxicated him. He began to look upon himself as made of superior clay to those about him. As last he said complacently: "I shall never be moved." Then, like a bolt from the blue, the blow fell. Before he could realize what was happening, the light had gone out of his sky, and life for him had toppled into ruins.

What had happened? Well, he who had gone for years without an ache or a pain suddenly found himself the prey of some disease. He went for the first time to consult a physician. The doctor looked him over, and his face went grave. "What's wrong?" the patient asked anxiously. But the doctor only shook his head. "But I demand to know," he persisted. Then the doctor told him. He passed death sentence upon him, telling him frankly that he must suffer and that there was no remedy but death. Then followed dreary days and nights of hopeless suffering during which he tried to be brave. But his efforts became more and more futile.

At last, in his bewilderment at God's perplexing ordering of things, he lost his faith. With physical and spiritual health gone a strange guest came into his home. That guest was weeping. He was not welcome, but he tarried none the less. He sat with him at every meal and by so doing, stole the taste from the most palatable of dishes. He even insisted upon sharing his bed with him. Therefore his nights were long and full of agony. And what made his situation utterly desperate was the dismal conviction that his unbidden guest must stay with him always.

But when all earthly hope was gone, he decided to make one last effort. Maybe the God who seemed to have forsaken him would help him even yet. Certainly, he felt, there ought to be one in a world like ours who could help when all human help had failed. So this sorely troubled man, this man whose physical tortures were almost forgotten in the presence of his tortures of soul, gave himself to prayer. He threw himself in his weakness into the Everlasting Arms, and God did not fail him. "He has turned for me my mourning into dancing," he sings proudly. "He came," he declares, "like a wise and tender nurse and removed my galling garment of sackcloth and decked me in a garment of gladness." And when he looked round for that unwelcome guest that he thought would never leave, lo, he found that he had gone, and that a new guest, songful joy, had come in his place. "And what God has done for me," he declares with assurance, "he will do for you. Weeping may tarry for a night, but joy cometh in the morning."

III

What is the good of this faith?

1. It keeps alive our hope. Keeping alive our hope, it also enables us to carry on with patient courage. It is hard to see things through with honor if hope is gone. Some manage it, but it is very difficult. But while some can carry on when hope is dead, many cannot. Sometime ago I looked into the face of one who

had committed suicide. It was a pathetic face. Why did he fling out of life? He lost hope. To-day was full of trouble and perplexity. Out ahead he saw a troop of to-morrows coming that looked as hopeless as to-day. Therefore he lost heart and gave over the fight. The night of weeping may be long and lonely, but we shall not turn coward and give up the battle if we are sure that joy is coming in the morning.

2. Not only will this faith give us hope and thereby minister to our courage and patient endurance, but it will be light to us during the night of our weeping. Such a faith will pluck sorrow's bitterest sting. What is it that makes our sorrow so bitter? It is our conviction of its finality, its irremediableness. If we could only feel that there is a cure, it would not be so hard. But the persistent refrain of sorrow is so often that of Poe's Raven, "Nevermore." The blow falls, and we look upon the ruins and sob, "The tender grace of a day that's dead will never come back to me." But how different it would be if we only believed that weeping is but temporary, that joy cometh in the morning.

Here, for instance, is a mother whose only laddie is gone from home. How still the house is and how desperately lonely! Then there is a knock at the door, a little slip of yellow paper is put into her hand. "Will be home to-morrow," it reads, and the name signed to it is that of her boy. A moment later the house is just as still and empty as it was before the message came. But in spite of that, the loneliness is gone from the mother's heart and a great joy has come in its place. And to you who are passing through a long night of weeping, I bring you a message. Hear it, and your heart will sing. A guest is coming to you. He is on his way. Soon he will turn the knob of your door and enter. Joy is coming in the morning. Nobody can be utterly cast down who believes that.

IV

But is such a faith possible for us who live in these perplexing days? This psalmist had been suffering from some deadly disease. He had been so close upon the gates of death that he was almost reckoned among the dead. In his desperate plight he had cried to God, and God had heard and healed. Can we, too, then believe that God will always heal the sick and suffering that cry to him? We cannot. There are those who pray just as earnestly as this poet, who, in spite of all their prayers, in spite of the prayers of those who love them, go quickly down to death. Then there are others who go on suffering for long, torturing years. Paul was such a one. He pleaded earnestly and insistently for the removal of his thorn, but his request was not granted.

But while God does not always see fit to give physical healing in answer to our prayers, he does something that is vastly better. He gives to him who really prays an inner strength, a calm courage that enables him to bear whatever load is laid upon him. He gives in answer to prayer a quiet heart, an abiding peace, a fullness of life that makes mere physical healing seem small and trifling. For it is possible to have the most vigorous of bodies and yet be a very weak and sickly soul. But our very bodily weakness that drives us to Christ becomes a source of spiritual strength. We learn with Paul that his grace is sufficient, and we shout with him: "Most gladly, therefore, will I rather glory in my infirmities that the power of Christ may rest upon me."

Then this text may have a richness of meaning for us to which even this psalmist himself was a stranger. Since his distant day Christ has come, bringing life and immortality to light through the gospel. We have heard him say: "Ye shall be sorrowful, but your sorrow shall be turned into joy." We believe that this is true in the here and now. We believe that it is going to be true in a finer and fuller sense in the dawning of that eternal morning to which he has encouraged us to look forward. "Let not your heart be troubled: ye believe in God, believe also in me. In my Father's house are many mansions: if it were not so, I would have told you." These are the words of our candid Christ. Since they are true we are safe in cherishing the wildest dreams for the future. In the presence of pain and change, in the presence of death itself we sing with calm confidence: "Joy cometh. It is coming now. It will come in its fullness, in the morning."

XIII

FAINTING

Psalm 27 : 13

"I had fainted, unless I had believed."

HERE is a man who realizes that he has had a very
close call. He has just succeeded in traversing a bit of
rugged road that threatened to work his ruin. More
than once had his knees gone weak. More than once
had the whole world seemed to grow black about him.
Again and again had he been on the point of toppling
over in a dead faint. But when he was reeling in his
tracks and ready to fall, there was one firm staff that
did not break in the grip of his clutching fingers.
There was one solid wall against which he leaned that
he found amply able to bear all the weight he could
put upon it. That wall was faith. So he won through;
but as he looks back over it all he declares with humility: "I had fainted, unless I had believed."

I

Now fainting is one of the most common and deadly
foes that you and I have to face. We know from our
own experiences what it is and something of the havoc
that it works. Sometime ago I was preaching in a
church that was greatly overcrowded. Suddenly a gen-

152

tleman who was standing in the rear of the building toppled over with a dull thud. The moment before he fainted he was, to all appearances, an eager and interested worshiper. He was making a worth-while contribution to the service. But as soon as he had fainted all this was over. There was no use to give him a hymn book; he would not sing. There was no use to pass him the collection plate; he could not give. There was no use to call him to prayer; he could not pray. There was no use to preach to him; he could not listen. Not only so, but four other men who had also been making their contribution to the service had to leave in order to look after him. Thus, by his fainting, he not only ceased to be an asset, but became a positive liability.

But for every one who faints physically there are literally scores who faint spiritually. How many such do we have in all our churches! Once they could be counted upon to be in their places at every service. Once the whole moral tone of the community was purified, in some measure, through their efforts. But all this is passed. The fires of their enthusiasm have gone out. Their interest has become listlessness. They are no longer a help, but a positive hindrance. They are no longer life-giving, they rather lie like huge stones across the mouth of the sepulcher where God is trying to raise some needy Lazarus from the dead. And this is the case, not because they have become openly antagonistic to the Church. It is the case not because they are vicious or flagrantly corrupt. It is rather the case because they have fainted.

A few years ago, over in a staid old city of Virginia, a lovely young couple stood before the altar to be married. They were of sufficient prominence socially for the event to be one of importance, not only to themselves, but to their community. All went well till the minister was about in the middle of the ceremony. Then his voice suddenly faltered, his ritual dropped from his fingers, and he himself toppled over into the palms. And there stood the embarrassed couple only half married. I rejoice to say that this minister was not so far gone that he could not be restored. Friends took him into the open air, and he was at last able to see his task through, "and they lived happily ever after."

But such tragedies do not always end so fortunately. In fact, because of our proneness to faint, our lives and our world are cluttered up with half-finished tasks. There are beautiful pictures that we never quite paint, books that we throw aside when we have written only the preface. There are fine goals from which we turn back when our pursuit has only begun. Near a certain Southern city there stood for years a very expensive building called "The Pink Palace." It was constructed of beautiful pink marble that had been brought from a distance of hundreds of miles. But in spite of all the wealth and labor that had been expended upon this palace, in spite of the beautiful material of which it was builded, it was not a poem, as it was surely meant to be. It was only a windowless ruin. This was the case because the builder fainted and gave over his task before he brought it to completion.

While I was pastor in Washington, D. C., I was sent one summer to the Canal Zone on a preaching and lecturing tour. Here and there, as we crossed the isthmus, I noticed great heaps of machinery that were slowly sinking into the mud and rusting away. Upon asking about these worthless heaps I was told that they had been left there by the French. Then I remembered that the French had undertaken to dig the canal and join these two seas. To that end they expended much money and not a few lives. But they did not see the task through. This was the case, not because they had proved the enterprise to be either undesirable or impossible, but rather because they fainted before their dream came true.

So we might go on endlessly. For of all cause of failure in every department of life there is none more sure than fainting. No wealth of opportunity, no gift of ability, even to the point of genius, can save us if we yield to this temptation. Had you and I been present when that famous race between the hare and the tortoise was run, who of us would have staked anything on the leaden-footed tortoise? But it was he that won, not because of his fleetness of foot, but because of his staying powers. Much of Edison's success is no doubt due to his keenness of intellect, but still more is due to his ability to hang on to the track of a dream with the tenacity of a bloodhound till he has made it a reality. If lack of opportunity and lack of ability have slain their thousands, fainting has slain its tens of thousands.

Since this is the case it is not to be wondered at that the writers of the Bible warn against fainting again and again. No more is it a matter of wonder that when they seek to show us the religious life at its very best, staying power, a stubborn refusal to faint, is one of its prominent characteristics. Possibly the finest word, for instance, that they have to say of Moses is that he endured. There was opposition, there was disappointment, there was bitter heartache, but he endured. Such stanchness, they felt, could only be accounted for in terms of God. So they said: "He endured as seeing him who is invisible." And they keep looking back to this same sturdy quality in Abraham. He had been lured into the unknown by a great dream that seemed destined never to come true. God had promised him much, but long years had slipped by and nothing had come of it. Springtime had gone, summer had gone, autumn had gone, and the gray days of winter were rapidly flying past. Still the promised heir had not come. But this stanch soul never gave up, never believed for a moment that God was going to let him down. "He staggered not at the promises," writes Paul with evident admiration. And refusing to faint, he at last realized his dream.

II

What are some of the causes of fainting?

1. A bad atmosphere. This causes us to faint physically. Even more often it causes us to faint spiritually. In fact, I doubt if we have ever rightly estimated
the power for good or evil of a right or wrong atmosphere. How almost inevitably we take on the spiritual
coloring of those about us! There are atmospheres
created by the individual and by the group that give
hope and help. Peter created such an atmosphere, according to The Acts, that his very shadow had healing
in it. There are homes that to enter is to be enriched.
It is to find one's self in an atmosphere in which it is
hard for a guilty thought to live. There are also
churches like that. The ushers remind us of inter-
preters at the House Beautiful. The people are friend-
ly, reverent, and worshipful. The minister and choir
seem possessed of good tidings. To enter such a service is to be made to say: "Surely God is in this place."
To be a part of such a congregation is to be enriched.
To be privileged to preach to such is to be lifted to the
heights.

But there are those who create an atmosphere that
chills like an east wind and bites like a killing frost.
I have preached in some churches whose congregations
by their prayers and sympathy lifted me on eagle wings.
I have preached in others and finished feeling as if
I never wanted to preach again. Beware of the at-

mosphere you create. Beware also of the atmosphere
with which you surround yourself through your asso-
ciates. If the group in which you spend your evenings
is one that treats with levity and contempt life's supreme values, if it ignores those fundamental integrities
by which the soul lives, then you are going to faint.
There are atmospheres in which a vitally religious life
is flatly impossible. Weak Herod made a little fight
against his soul with the blood of John the Baptist.
But he had put himself in a bad atmosphere, therefore
he failed. "For the sake of them that sat with him at
meat, he commanded it to be given her." The wise
man had in mind the power for evil of a bad atmosphere when he said: "The companion of fools shall be
destroyed."

2. Some faint at the sight of blood. One day a
young enthusiast came to Jesus with the finest of all
possible purposes in his heart. "Lord," he said, "I
will follow thee whithersoever thou goest." Nothing
could be finer than that. But Jesus did not thrill. He
knew that the young man did not understand all that
was involved in his promise. Therefore he told him
that he himself was more homeless than the foxes, that
he might have to sleep supperless upon the mountain
side. He showed him a cross with a bit of crimson
upon it, and at that he who was all eagerness fell into
a dead faint. While he yearned for the goods, the
price was greater than he was willing to pay. It is too
often the case. Some of you are not in the fight, not

because the call of Christ makes no appeal, but rather
because you are afraid of a little bloodletting. Therefore you say whiningly: "But for these vile guns, I
would have been a soldier."

3. We faint from weakness. Sometimes our weakness is natural. Sometimes it is the result of utter
weariness. That was one of the causes that led Elijah
to faint. After his victory at Mount Carmel, he trotted
some seventeen miles to Jezreel, then a day's journey
into the wilderness. He was tired when he began.
He was utterly exhausted when he reached the familiar
shades of the juniper tree. Christ's way of life is not
one of case. It is not a drifting with the current, but
a breasting of it. At times we get tired of being good,
feel in our very hearts that we should like to fling up
the whole business, rush back to the leeks and garlic
of Egypt, and go our own heedless and selfish ways.

Then we sometimes faint from weakness that is
brought on by lack of food. When Richard Mansfield
was struggling to win success on the stage, he was
also having a hard fight with poverty. One night, in
the midst of his act, he fell in a dead faint. The cause
of his fainting was weakness born of hunger. Many of
the saints have fainted for this same reason. They
have forgotten that their spiritual needs are just as
pressing as the physical. It was the realization of this
that enabled Mr. Stedfast to win where so many others
have failed. "His Word," he declares, "did I use to
gather as an antidote against my faintings." Beware

of the starving of the soul. It ends in moral and spiritual collapse.

4. Others, still, faint from chastisement. The writer of the Hebrews was facing this fact when he said: "My son, despise not thou the chastening of the Lord, nor faint when thou art rebuked of him." I have seen people faint through sheer suffering. Sometimes it came in the guise of a material loss that left a howling wolf of want where there had once been luxury. At other times it came as hopeless physical pain where there had been buoyant and abounding health. At other times, still, there was the loss of one unspeakably dear that seemed to leave life far more bare than the boughs of a tree stripped by the rude winds of winter. Some grow more sweet and strong under sorrow, but others faint under it.

5. The final cause of fainting I mention is discouragement. This is possibly the most fruitful of them all. I read sometime ago of a man who lost his life in a blizzard in one of our middle-western States. When they found the body it was only a few feet from his own door. No doubt he fought hard before he allowed himself to sleep the sleep of death. But it was night, and he could not see how near home he was. I feel sure that had he only known, he would have gone those few remaining steps. He fainted, in part, from loss of hope. Certainly that is the secret of the failure of multitudes who undertake the Christian life. They struggle and fail, till at last they allow themselves

to become convinced that real sainthood is beyond their reach; that, whatever others may have made of the high and exacting business, for themselves it is a sheer futility. Thus they become discouraged and faint.

III

But in spite of all the temptations to faint by which this sturdy saint was surrounded, he somehow managed to stand firm. "I had fainted," he tells us frankly, "unless I had believed." But he refused to surrender his faith. In the face of difficulties he kept believing. Thus he came through all his tempestuous trials with honor. What, then, did he believe? Upon what rugged convictions did he stand to find them as the very Rock of Ages under his feet?

1. He believed in the Church. It is evident that this psalmist had found strength in the worship of the sanctuary. He was zealous and faithful in his attendance upon the services of his Church. He might have gone for varied reasons, but this was supreme: That he might behold the beauty of the Lord. In these services he somehow won his way past all that was outward and visible till he came face to face with God. In the strength born of this vision, he was able "to walk and not be weary and to run and not faint."

2. He believed in prayer. He had learned to wait on God. "When I was sorely tempted to faint, I found strength to stand through prayer. You will find that it will work in your case," he declares with quiet confi-

dence. "Wait on the Lord; be of good courage, and he shall strengthen thine heart; wait, I say, on the Lord." Those who pray do have a strength to which the prayerless must remain strangers. Jesus, you remember, spoke a parable "to the end, that men ought always to pray, and not to faint." He did not believe that praying and fainting could live in the same heart at the same time. In the Garden he gave himself to prayer and won the fight. His disciples came to their ordeal prayerless, and for this reason they came to it powerless. Here is a little merchant vessel that has been for weary days and nights the plaything of the storm. All on board have fainted except one. "All hope," says the story, "that we should be saved was taken away." Then comes a man of prayer to cry: "Be of good cheer." Through the strength born of prayer he refused to faint and thus saved both himself and those that sailed with him.

3. He had faith in the final triumph of righteousness. There is nothing more weakening than the belief that we are fighting for a losing cause. There is nothing more bracing than the conviction that, all appearances to the contrary notwithstanding, we are sure to win. Did not our Lord strengthen himself with this conviction? "Who for the joy that was set before him," the joy of victory, the joy of drawing all men unto himself, "endured the cross, despising the shame." It is with this same faith that Paul is seeking to strengthen us when he says: "And let us not be weary in well

doing, for in due season we shall reap, if we faint not." No seed of goodness sown ever comes to naught. Tares will grow if we plant them. But so will roses and violets. "I had fainted unless I had believed" that no life invested on the side of right can ever fail. But, because I believe, I will fight on to the victorious end.

XIV

THE GREAT THIRST

Psalm 42 : 1

"As the hart panteth after the water brooks, so panteth my soul after thee, O God."

I

YEARS ago as a lad I was working one day in a field on the back side of my father's farm. This field was washed by the songful waters of the Buffalo River. Away in the distance on the opposite side of the farm stood a range of rugged and majestic hills. Suddenly from among these hills I heard the baying of a pack of hounds. My attention was all the more alert because we ourselves did not keep hounds. As I listened the baying became more and more distinct. By this I knew that the pack was coming toward me. Then as I waited in expectation I was startled to see a deer suddenly come into view. The pursuing hounds were dreadfully close upon his heels. It was easy to see that the poor creature was almost spent. But on he came, running desperately for his life. Then as he saw me in his path, in an effort to turn, he dropped to his knees. Immediately the hounds had their cruel fangs at his throat and the long chase was over.

164

Why was this deer running in my direction? It was
not that he expected any help at my hands. He was
as fearful of me as of the hounds that hung upon his
heels. He was running toward me because he was
making for the river that lay just behind me. That
brook offered everything to this poor spent creature. It
offered escape from the deadly foes that were thirsting
for his blood. It offered rest for his body that was
wearied by long hours of desperate running. It offered
satisfaction for his burning thirst. It offered life itself.
"If I can only reach this brook," he might have said to
himself, "I shall live. I shall again have an opportunity to realize my destiny in the glad freedom of my
native hills." No wonder, therefore, that this poor,
pursued hart was panting for the water brook.

Now the psalmist tells us that his own pathetic plight
is close akin to that of this hounded deer. He, too,
is being pursued by bitter foes. They have chased
him into exile. Even now they are taunting him with
the derisive question, "Where is thy God?" And the
bitterest heartache of it all is that he can give no answer to their question that is satisfying even to himself. Once he feels that he could have done so. In
those glad yesterdays when he was privileged to take
part in the religious festivities of his people he was
quite sure of God. But it is not so now. His realization of him is no longer vivid. And since sorrow's
crown of sorrow is remembering happier days, his soul
is cast down within him. In his bitterness he tells us

that his tears have been his food day and night.   He feels that he must have help.   He simply cannot get on without it.

But where does he turn in his hour of desperation? What fountain does he seek for the slaking of his thirst?   He turns to One that he believes can do for him what the water brook can do for the deer, and far more.   What place does the brook fill in the program of the deer?   It is a great luxury, but it is more than a luxury.   It is an absolute necessity.   And what place does God fill in the program of the psalmist?   He leaves us in no doubt as to the answer to that question. He counts God as an absolute necessity.   There is simply no getting on without him.   Therefore he cries after him as a hungry, frightened child might cry after its mother: "My soul thirsteth for God, for the living God: when shall I come and appear before God?"

II

Now according to the Bible, the thirst of this poet is not unique.   On the contrary, it is universal.   It belongs to all mankind.   Just as these bodies of ours are not self-sustaining, but must be watered and fed from resources external to themselves, even so it is with our souls.   If our bodies do not have physical bread and water, they will hunger and thirst and die. Just so, if our souls do not have God, the Bread of Life and the Water of Life, they, too, will hunger and thirst and die.   Jesus says very plainly, "Whosoever

drinketh of this water shall thirst again." That is, no
man can be satisfied by a well of his own contriving.
No water that this world has to offer can meet the
needs of these immortal spirits of ours. Every man,
therefore, is either consciously or unconsciously thirsting after God. This is a characteristic of the race.

Jesus discovers to us this thirst for God on the part
of men and women that we should have considered the
least likely to possess it. For instance, he tells of a
youth that once grew sick and tired of the restraints of
home. He became disgusted with the very things that
should have been his keenest joy. Finally he ruthlessly
shook the gentle hand of his father from his shoulder,
flung away from it all, and went into a far country.
But somehow he did not find what he expected to find.
His adventure did not turn out well. Instead of winning satisfaction he only won the opposite. He was
reduced to utter want. In his dire poverty he was
forced to accept the lowly position of swineherd. The
hogs that he tended were quite contented. They were
well satisfied with the husks that he fed them. But no
such satisfaction was possible for himself. He had
hungers that these husks could not satisfy. He had
thirsts that no fountains of the far country could slake.
He was tormented by the memory of dear dead dreams
and of old loved faces. At last he could stand it no
longer. His very hungers and thirsts scourged him
back into his father's arms.

Then one day when Jesus was resting upon an old

well curb, he saw a woman coming to him through the noonday heat. She had made a ghastly wreck of life, poor soul. Perhaps she had been beautiful once. Even yet she is witty and well able to give a good account of herself in an argument. But she has squandered her supreme treasure and is now seemingly nothing more than an utter moral and spiritual bankrupt. She is coming to the well at this sultry and unseemly hour, doubtless because she dreads the hot rays of the sun less than the hot words of her more decent and respectable sisters. Of course she is hopeless. Everybody said as much. She is not only a thing of shame in the eyes of those who know her best, but she is content to be so.

But Jesus sees with different eyes. As he looks into her empty life he discovers what would doubtless have been a bit of a surprise even to herself. He sees that she is really hungry and thirsty for God. He tells her frankly that the one reason that she does not change that well curb into an altar of penitence and prayer is, not that she is satisfied to be the thing that she is, but rather that she is not sure that she can ever be different. If she could only be made to see the door that is open before her, with what amazing eagerness she would rush out of her sordid prison into the freedom of a new life. "If thou knewest the gift of God, and who it is that saith to thee, give me to drink, thou wouldest have asked of him, and he would have given thee living water." Yes, even in this outcast woman, who was

looked upon by the respectable Jew as lower than a
street dog, there was a deathless hunger after God.

Again Jesus tells of a certain farmer of his acquaintance who had made a great success. Everything he
touched seemed to turn to gold. This year his crops
are so abundant that he does not have room in which
to store them. He has to tear down his old barns and
build greater. Surely life for him is full. To the
onlooker there seems nothing to be desired. But no,
he is not content. He discovers, as millions of others
have done, that things never satisfy. Full barns may
prove sufficient for his donkeys, but they are not quite
enough for himself. Therefore we find him saying
fretfully and peevishly to himself, "Soul, thou hast
much goods laid up for many years; . . . eat, drink,
and be merry." But his soul turns from it all with
loathing and disgust. And here again we find tormenting hungers and burning thirsts.

This contention on the part of the Scriptures that
thirst for God is universal is also supported by the
facts of experience. What is more evident to-day than
the restlessness and the discontent of the vast majority
of the people we know? We can read it in their very
faces as we pass them on the street. How few there
are out of whose eyes looks "the peace of a great discovery." Poor people are discontented, but the rich
are quite as much so. The ignorant are discontented,
but often the cultured are even more so. This fretful
fever belongs to no one class. It belongs to all classes,

to the old and to the young, to those in harsh circumstances and to those who live upon the sunny side of the street.

> "We look before and after,
>   And pine for what is not;
> Our sincerest laughter
>   With some pain is fraught;
> Our sweetest songs are those
>   That tell of saddest thought."

"Vanity of vanities," says Thackeray as he brings his greatest novel to its close, "Vanity of vanities! Who of us gets his desire, or getting it, is satisfied."

But, in saying that thirst for God is universal, we do not mean to declare that every man is conscious of the fact that he is thirsting for God. This is by no means the case. Should you suggest as much to many a feverish soul, there would be a quick and hot denial. Such a one fancies that God is the very least and last object of his thirst. What he is really thirsting for is for something tangible, solid, substantial. What he needs to satisfy him is a better position or a better house or a faster car. What he needs is to get a divorce, or to get the Eighteenth Amendment repealed or to get "somewhere east of Suez where the best is like the worst." What he needs is success, more money, a heaven made up of things. But the fact that such a one does not know that for which he thirsts does not discount the fact that his real thirst is for God.

Here is a wee laddie asleep in his bed. By and by

he wakens and begins to wail. We come at once to his assistance and give him one toy after another in an effort to quiet him. But in spite of our well-meaning efforts he only wails the louder. "What is the matter?" we cry in desperation. He does not tell us. He simply wails louder still. Now the real trouble is that the little fellow is hungry. He does not know what the matter is himself, nor does he know for what he hungers. But in spite of his ignorance the moment he finds his way into his mother's arms his outcry ceases. Now, the fact that he did not know that for which he hungered did not lessen his discomfort in the least, nor did it prevent his satisfaction when his wants were met.

That was a rather queer and ugly creature that a mother hen hatched along with her brood of normal and respectable chicks. The egg from which it came had been found on the side of a rugged mountain. He seemingly did his best to satisfy himself with the tame, unexciting life of the barnyard. But somehow it did not work. His crooked beak was out of place there, and his great wings seemed utterly useless. So the poor, awkward thing looked on his drab world with lackluster eyes. He did not fit in and was very evidently not at home. But one day he heard a wild scream above him. He looked up, and his eyes kindled. He saw a great bird like himself, an eagle. Then he realized what he had been thirsting for all the while. Therefore he spread his burnished brown wings and was away to the freedom of his larger world. He was

made for the cloudland and for the crags of the mountains.   Therefore he could not be satisfied in the barnyard.   No more can we be satisfied with less than God.
This is true whether we ever recognize it or not.

Nor are we to assume that, because this thirst for
God is universal, it is always the same in its intensity.
Such is not the case.   There are some sluggish souls
for whom this longing may be quite vague.   There are
those, who, while discontented with the barnyard life,
manage to get through on such low levels, with at least
a partial degree of satisfaction.   But there are other
fine, sensitive souls for whom this thirst is a gnawing
agony, a poignant pain.   Such was the case with our
author.   Such has been the case with an innumerable
company.   But whether we thirst consciously or unconsciously, whether vaguely or intensely, God has planted
within every human heart a deathless hunger and thirst
for himself.

III

Now just as universal as is this thirst after God,
just so universal is the satisfaction offered for it
through the riches of grace if Christ Jesus our Lord.
It is largely to emphasize and compel our faith in this
great truth, it would seem, that the Bible was written.
One witness after another comes forward to bear eager
testimony to the fact that God has fully met his needs.
Here, for instance, is the author of the one hundred and
seventh Psalm.   He has known something of the agony

of a burning thirst, even as you and I. But he has found his way to the spring. Therefore he shouts the good news to you and me. "He satisfieth the longing soul."

And Isaiah in his day saw the hot and restless crowds about him hurry from one booth to another and buy and buy, only to come away in the end the more restless and dissatisfied. At last, when he could endure the tragedic sight no longer, he cried after them: "Ho, every one that thirsteth, come ye to the waters, and he that hath no money; come ye, buy and eat; yea, come, buy wine and milk without money and without price. Wherefore do ye spend money for that which is not bread? and your labor for that which satisfieth not? Harken diligently unto me, and eat ye that which is good, and let your soul delight itself in fatness." "Why pay your last penny for what can never satisfy," he asks in bewilderment, "when he who meets your needs may be had for the taking?" Why indeed? But with a veritable passion for being cheated, we keep up the sorry business from generation to generation.

> "Earth gets its price for what Earth gives us,
>   The beggar is taxed for a corner to die in,
> The priest hath his pay who comes and shrives us,
>   We bargain for the graves we lie in;
> At the devil's booth are all things sold,
> Each ounce of dross costs its ounce of gold;
> For a cap and bells our lives we pay,
>   Bubbles we buy with a whole soul's tasking,
> 'Tis heaven alone that is given away,
>   'Tis only God may be had for the asking."

This claim that God can satisfy every man's need becomes, if possible, even more emphatic upon the pages of the New Testament. It reaches its climax in the magnificent and daring appeals of Jesus. With what sublime audacity he flings out this invitation, "If any man thirst, let him come to me and drink." If any man—there is no single exception. He claims to be able to meet every man's need regardless of who that man is or what his circumstances may be. "I am the bread of life," he declares again, "he that cometh to me shall never hunger; and he that believeth on me shall never thirst. . . . But whosoever drinketh of the water that I shall give him shall never thirst; but the water that I shall give him shall be in him a well of water springing up into everlasting life." And those who have accepted this invitation have never been disappointed. Countless millions through the centuries have been able to sing out of their own experiences:

"I heard the voice of Jesus say, 'Behold, I freely give
  The living water; thirsty one, stoop down, and drink, and live.'
  I came to Jesus, and I drank of that life-giving stream;
  My thirst was quenched, my soul revived, and now I live in him."

And mark you, this satisfaction means something more than individual salvation. It means that of course. "Thou shalt be like a watered garden," sings the prophet. A garden—that is, something that is cultivated, fenced in, cared for. It must be watered from without. It is not sufficient to water itself. Its flowers

wither, its beauties die unless it is watered. And man
is that garden. And God is the One who supplies him
with water. But that is not all. This same prophet
adds, "He shall be like a spring whose waters fail not."
That is, the heart that has found satisfaction in God
becomes a means of bringing that same benediction to
others. Jesus was speaking to the same purpose when
he said: "If any man thirst, let him come to me, and
drink. He that believeth on me, as the scripture hath
said, out of his belly shall flow rivers of living water."

Now the poor, spent deer, of which I spoke at the
beginning of my message, never reached the brook.
He was too tired. The hounds were too near. The
brook was too far away. Then, too, there was somebody in his way. So he died with his goal unreached,
his thirst unsatisfied. But it need not be so with you
and me. Our God is not far away. He is infinitely
near. He is closer than our foes. He is as near as our
burning thirst. Nor do we have to wait for some far-
off to-morrow to find him. He is ready to meet our
needs in the here and now. And nobody can rob us
of our finding him but ourselves. This is his amazing
claim. Shall we take him seriously and drink and live,
or shall we go on our feverish way feeling that his
promise is altogether too good to be true?

There is an old story of a derelict ship whose crew
was starving for water. At last another ship came into
sight. This distressed crew signaled, "Water, water;
we are starving for water." "Let down your buckets

where you are," came back the surprising answer. But such an answer seemed to these starving men nothing less than bitter mockery. So they signaled again, "Water, water; we are starving for water." Again there came back the same answer, "Let down your buckets where you are." At last they complied, not at all sure that anything would come of it, but with a dim hope that possibly they were not being mocked. And something did come of it. They found a supply of fresh water that to them was measureless. For, unknown to themselves, they had been driven into the wide mouth of the Amazon, whose waters freshen the sea for many miles from the shore. And this is Christ's call to you and me. He is not mocking. Let down your buckets where you are, and you, too, will find that he satisfieth the longing soul.

XV

A NEW SONG

Psalm 40: 3

"He hath put a new song in my mouth."

HERE is a word to interest the most listless. However drowsy we are, this text ought to rouse us into eager wakefulness. However hopeless we are, it ought to startle us into glad expectation. It is a word that is needed in every age. It is especially needed by the jaded generation of which we are a part. Life has grown old for many of us. In spite of all our facilities for thrills, we are finding the business of living rather stale and unexciting. "What has been will be, and there is no new thing under the sun," said a tired and bored cynic many years ago. To this pessimistic declaration many of us are ready to give a hearty "Amen." Instead of finding new songs we have found old yawns. Or if there has been any music at all, too often it has been a jarring jazz that has left us the more weary and disillusioned. But here is one who has discovered a new song. Life for him is not in the sear and yellow leaf; it is in the full flush of spring. He has therefore a story to tell that we greatly need to hear.

What is the source of this new song? From what fountain of inspiration does it flow?

This song is not a child of chance. No more is it a creature of circumstances. It is not merely a song of youth, for instance. There is nothing to indicate that this poet is singing simply because he is brushing the dewy flowers of life's morning. Even though such were the case, we know well enough that youth cannot always be depended upon to be an inspirer of song. Sometimes youth sings, but very often it does not. Many of our youth to-day seem to find life quite as drab and insipid as those of us who are in middle life, or as those who are nearing the sunset. In fact, some of the most weary and listless souls that I meet are young men and women who have not yet got out of their twenties. Some even seem thoroughly "fed up" on life who are on the springtime side of twenty. Therefore, to look to youth as a sure inspiration of song is to look to a source that is thoroughly unreliable.

No more does this song have its rise in the hills of prosperity and worldly success. There is no slightest hint, in the first place, that this poet had found either fame or fortune. Nor is there anywhere proof that the prosperous find life more songful than the failures. Some years ago I was entertained in the home of a man whose wealth amounted to many millions. During the afternoon the husband and wife took me for a drive over the city. When we came back, as we were getting out of the car, in spite of the fact that company was present, the wife burst into tears. She was a woman of an assured place in society. She seemed to possess all that heart could wish. She lived in a palace, yet, as I have thought of that home in after years, I have thought of it not so much as a place of songs as a place of sobs. We can safely say, therefore, that the song of this psalmist is not born of circumstances. No abiding song ever is.

Neither is he singing because he is possessed of a rugged determination. There are times that we sing from a sense of duty. We feel that for the sake of others it is the helpful thing to do, and in this we are right. There is something finely heroic about the man that refuses to parade his sorrow, but rather locks it all in his heart and smiles on the world. It requires a high type of courage to keep a song upon the lips while there is a sob in the heart. Yet there are those big and brave enough for this taxing task. This was a practice that we urged with great enthusiasm during the stressful days of the World War. We sang lustily, "Pack up your troubles in your old kit bag, and smile, smile, smile." And some of us did it, though the smile sometimes changed into a grimace the moment we were alone.

That is an appealing picture that Moore gives of the young woman who loved the Irish patriot, Robert Emmet. Emmet, as you know, was executed in his early manhood for his too great zeal for his native land. But he died like a hero, and the girl who loved him tried hard to show herself as courageous in the bearing of her sorrow as he had been in the laying down of his life. The task, however, was too heavy for her. She went away to Italy to recover her failing health. There, in spite of all her heroic efforts, she faded like a flower.

> "She is far from the land where her young hero sleeps,
>   And lovers around her are sighing;
> But sadly she turns from their gaze and weeps,
>   For her heart in the grave is lying.
>
> She sings the wild songs of her dear native plains,
>   Every note that he loved awaking;
> Ah! little they think who delight in her strains
>   How the heart of the minstrel is breaking.
>
> He had lived for his love, for his country he died,
>   They were all that to life had entwined him;
> Nor soon shall the tears of his country be dried,
>   Nor long shall his love stay behind him.
>
> Oh! Make her a home where the sunbeams rest,
>   When they promise a glorious to-morrow;
> They'll shine o'er her sleep like a smile from the west,
>   From her own loved island of sorrow."

She sang, but while her song concealed her broken heart it did not heal it. This new song of our psalmist is born of something even finer than a heroic determination.

What, then, is the source of his song? It is a gift

of God. "He hath put a new song in my mouth," declares this poet joyously. Then his song has a fountain source that is abiding. His music need never be hushed into silence nor changed into discord. On the farm where I lived as a boy there is one of the loveliest springs that ever sang its way out of the hills. We call it the Basin Spring. "The trees fold their green arms around it, trees a century old, and the winds go whispering through them and the sunbeams drop their gold." The waters of this spring used to flow over a large flat rock. But one day hands that have probably been dust for centuries chiseled a basin upon the face of this rock. That basin, even in times of severest drought, is always filled to overflowing. This is the case because it has water constantly flowing into it from an unfailing reservoir among the great hills. And so it is with the music of this joyous singer. His song is born of the inexhaustible resources that are locked in the heart of God.

II

What is the nature of this poet's song?

1. His is a song of deliverance. "He brought me up also out of a horrible pit, out of the miry clay." How he ever got into this pit we are not told. He may have been plunged into it through some great and devastating calamity. He may have fallen into it through his own willfulness or carelessness or spiritual stupidity. But regardless of how he had come to be

there, there he was, and there was no shutting his eyes
to his tragic situation. He could never forget the stark
horror of it all. The place was dark and cold. It was
unspeakably lonely and as silent as death itself. And
that which brought his awful plight to the very climax
of hopelessness and despair was that he could find no
solid resting place for his feet. For this pit did not
have firm masonry for its floor. It did not even have
water. It only had stenchful mire that gripped him
with tenacious fingers and slowly dragged him into a
ghastly grave.

It is Victor Hugo, I think, that tells the story of a
man caught in the quicksand. One moment this man is
walking in safety. Then his path begins to cling to
his feet a bit. A few more steps and he is bogged
down to his knees. He then begins to struggle frantically. But the more he struggles, the deeper he sinks.
Soon the treacherous sand has reached his waist. By
this time the unfortunate victim has become desperate.
He now realizes that he is being slowly swallowed by
a hideous, blind mouth that is absolutely without mercy.
He cries for help, but there is no response. He looks
at the clouds floating in the blue and the birds as they
soar above his head, and they seem to mock him. He
prays, he shrieks, he curses. He struggles with every
ounce of his energy, but the implacable mouth still
swallows him only the faster. At last his final wild
wail ends in a gulp. The cruel sand has filled his
mouth, and the futile struggle is over.

Now the singer tells us that he was like this man, that he, too, was sinking and was horribly sure that all was over, that he, too, cried desperately for help. But here he has a different story to tell. There was One that answered his cry. He stretched up a helpless hand, and that hand was seized by One that was mighty, and he felt himself lifted to safety. Since then he has had a song upon his lips. It is a song of deliverance. Some of us can join him in the singing of it, for such a song befits the lips of every man who has greatly sinned and who has been greatly saved. Such a song is even more fitting for the lips of those who, through being reared in Christian homes and through the guidance of Christian parents, have been spared the agony of falling into the horrible pit out of which this poet had to be rescued, at what a cost both to himself and to his Lord.

2. Then this song of our poet is a song of security. "He hath set my feet upon a rock, and established my goings." This marvelously delivered man walks to-day with an assured confidence. His confidence, however, is not born of his faith in himself, but of his faith in God. It is God who has enabled him to say with the prophet, "He hath made my feet like hinds' feet." He has given him a bracing sense of security. He has made it possible for him to sing with the author of the twenty-third Psalm, "Yea, though I walk through the valley of the shadow of death, I will fear no evil." His footing is firm and secure. He does not look to

to-morrow with feverish fear as he once did. The old horror is gone, and he can now look ahead with quiet eyes, knowing that the God who keeps him to-day will be sufficient for him to-morrow.

3. This song is also a song of gratitude. In the consciousness of the deliverance and security that God in his goodness had given him he could not withhold his praise. He burst into song as naturally as the bird that "lets his illumined being o'errun, with the deluge of summer it receives." We are not so grateful as we ought to be, any of us. One day Jesus healed ten lepers. Having been healed, nine of them hurried upon their separate ways, utterly forgetful of the healer. Only one came back with a song of praise upon his lips. Too often we join the nine. Too rarely we join the one. This psalmist is among those who came back. His is a song of thanksgiving.

4. Finally this song is winsomely and fascinatingly new. Its newness, however, is not born of the fact that this singer is saying something that has never been said before. It is not a bizarre song; it is a new song. I am glad that this is the case. There is no real virtue however, in mere novelty. Neither new songs nor new gospels are needed, if by new we mean only the unusual and the novel. I recently heard a wise preacher say to a group of theological graduates: "My young friends, when you begin to preach and one comes forward at the close of the service to say to you, 'That was a new thought you gave me to-day, I never thought of that

before,' don't be too elated over it. The chances are that he will never think of it again." This song is new, not because it is merely queer, but because it is born of experiences that are new and vital to the singer.

Yesterday a hearse passed you on the street. You only gave it a brief glance. A hearse is such a common sight. Yet to some who followed, that journey to the cemetery was as new and poignant as if they were the first who had ever been called upon to bury their dead out of their sight. The other day I heard a young mother talking to her first baby. She was saying the same sweet, ungrammatical nothings that generations of mothers have said. Yet they were fascinatingly new and lovely. They were born of experience. And here is a man and a maiden who have come to love each other. In their own ears how amazingly new and startling are the things they say. Yet they have been said over and over again countless millions of times. Recently a mother found an old letter that was so sentimental that she told her daughter frankly she was ashamed of her for writing such a letter. But when the daughter looked it over she found to her delight it was not her letter at all, but her mother's. Love talks the same language through the centuries, but it is always fascinatingly new.

Jesus said: "Every scribe instructed unto the kingdom of heaven is like unto a man that is an householder, which bringeth forth out of his treasure things new and old." That is what this psalmist is doing.

That is what we can do. If we have a fresh, **vital**
experience of God, our song will be as new and fresh
as the first rose of June, yet as old as the ordered coming of the seasons. It will be as new as the first smile
that dimples the cheek of the mother's first baby boy,
yet it will be as old as motherhood. That was an old
sky into which Shelley's skylark flew, but the bird
looked at it as if his were the first eyes that had ever
seen it, and as he looked he sang a song so new that
the poet had to exclaim,

> "Teach me half the gladness
> That thy brain must know,
> Such harmonious madness
> From my lips would flow,
> The world should listen then,
> As I am listening now."

Just so long as we are making new discoveries in God,
so long will our song be enchantingly new.

III

Now what is the good of this new song? Why
should we covet it ourselves?

1. It is an unspeakable benediction to him who pos-
sesses it. Song means joy, laughter, gladness. Our
present-day religion is a bit short on joy. Therefore it
is short on power. "The joy of the Lord is your
strength." It is a source of strength in our hours of
bereavement. It is a source of strength when our
dreams fail to come true. It is a steady staff upon

which to lean when the rain is on the roof and the light has gone out of the skies. It is a strong anchor when the fierce tempest toys with our bark and "sorrow sits sobbing like a troubled ghost in every chamber of the heart."

Then it is a source of strength in our times of temptation. There are those who, in some measure, can resist the downward tug through sheer force of will. There are others who may be able to get past the death-haunted shores where the sirens sing by the poor expedient of stuffing wool into their ears. But the method of Ulysses was far better. He took on board with him one whose song was so much more winsome than that of the sirens that the music of those death-dealing creatures lost its spell. This is a sure way of victory for ourselves. The most luring songs that the world can sing will lose their spell and become mere jarring discord if we have singing in our hearts the new song of the psalmist.

2. This new song is not only a benediction to the singer, but to his fellows as well. "Many shall see it, sings our poet, and fear, and shall trust in the Lord." "Many shall see it." Does not the poet use the wrong word? Should he not have said, "Many shall hear it"? Who sees a song? Yet so it stands written. And you doubtless recall the wise conclusion that John Milton reached when, as a lad, he dreamed of writing a poem that the world would not willingly let die. He declared that he who would write a great

poem must himself be a poem. And our singer has attained in some measure the high standard set by Milton. With this new song upon his lips that is but an echo of the song within his heart, he has himself become a song. There is a winsomeness and charm about his life that may be seen as well as heard. He is so in tune with the Infinite that those whose lives he touches cannot resist his spell. They yearn to know his secret, and, knowing it, they, too, come to trust in the Lord.

We who profess to be Christians are often dreadfully short on winsomeness. We read of some of the early saints that great grace was upon them. That is, they were gracious, fascinating, appealing. To associate with them was to become keen and eager to find what they had found. But when the Pharisee had finished thanking God that he was not as other men, I wonder who followed him home to ask him about the deep things of the soul. I wonder who went to him to inquire wistfully how they, too, might separate themselves from the unwashed crowd of "extortioners, unjust, adulterers" and become faultless and unstained like himself. I wonder what man came with eager step and with an impassioned appeal that would take no denial to learn how he might rise to the sublime height of fasting twice a week. You know. No man came. And it was not because this Pharisee was not religious. It was rather because he was horribly religious. He was not in tune with God, and there was no wooing harmony in his life.

Ole Bull, you remember, had a friend, Leif Ericson by name, who claimed that he had no ear for music. The fact that the violin of his fellow countryman had an angel-choir hidden within it mattered nothing to him. The fact that Ole Bull could change his bow into a magic wand and make tempests crash and thunder, or birds sing, or brooks leap and prattle as songfully as the laughter of a happy child, did not interest Leif Ericson in the least. He even refused to go and hear Ole Bull play. But the great violinist won him in the end. How did he go about it? He did not crash his violin over his friend's head. He did not lecture him. He did not tell what the man who is not moved by concord of sweet sounds is fit for. He went down to where Leif was working and played for him; played with all the power of his compelling genius. And what was the result? It is easy to guess. Leif's heart became warm, his face softened, and his eyes grew big with tears. And then and there the soul of this scientist and inventor was taken captive by the charm of music.

It is even so that this singer of the new song seeks to take captive the hearts of men. He knows that we are not going to win the world by our wails. We are not going to win by our complaints. We are not going to win by persistently prating about what is wrong with the Church. We are not going to win by proclaiming what a distressingly hard time we are having as we try to serve the Lord. We are not going to win by discordant lives that clash like violins played out of tune. But we can win through the appealing winsomeness of lives in tune with the Christ. If there is a harmony about our lives that the world cannot give and cannot take away, somebody is going to ask the secret. We are very short on inner music. We are sadly lacking in freshness and newness. If we show the way to the new song by the beauty and charm of our lives, "many shall see it, and fear, and shall trust in the Lord."

XVI

THE GOODNESS OF GOD

Psalm 34: 3

"O magnify the Lord with me, and let us exalt his name together."

THIS sunny singer has a wooing word upon his lips. He is not abusive. He is not undertaking to prod us. He is not setting himself to the task of driving us out to church. He is resolved that he himself will go. He is bent upon having a praise service. In fact, the giving of thanks is to be henceforth a fixed habit with him. Every day is to be a thanksgiving day. "I will bless the Lord at all times," he sings happily. "His praise shall continually be in my mouth." He is eager that we share his gratitude; so he knocks on our doors, lays eager hands upon us, and says cheerfully, "O magnify the Lord with me, and let us exalt his name together."

I

Why is this man so full of gratitude? Why is it that for him to open his mouth is to burst forth into spontaneous praise? It is not because his circumstances are perfect. This Psalm is thought by some to have been written by David while he was in hiding

191

from Saul. But whether this is the case or not, the author, whoever he is, faces the fact that circumstances are often against us. "Many are the afflictions of the righteous," he tells us frankly. He is wise enough to know that if we wait till everything is perfectly to our liking before we give thanks then we are likely to wait forever. Do you remember that wonderful palace of which we read in the *Arabian Nights?* It was a veritable dream of loveliness. The owner was naturally exceedingly proud of it. One day he was showing its marvelous wealth and beauty to a friend. When this friend had looked it over he said: "Yes, it is wonderful, it is almost perfect. All that is needed is a roc's egg to swing from the ceiling." But the owner of the palace did not know what a roc was, nor did he know that it laid eggs. Naturally he did not know where its eggs were if it did lay. So his friend left him in wretchedness and bitter discontent. His palace was little better than a prison without a roc's egg to swing from the ceiling and thus make it perfect.

Nor is this man grateful because of any goodness or greatness he sees in himself. He is boasting, but he is not boasting of his own achievements. We do not like boasting that is born of self-importance. Such boasting is bad taste. It is a mark of conceit. It is thoroughly offensive. But not so the boasting of this joyous singer. "My soul shall make her boast in the Lord." I could wish that we had a congregation made up of such boasters. I could wish that we might have a city full of them. I could wish that we might have a world of them. Such boasters do not offend; they delight. They do not make us sad; they make us glad. "My soul shall make her boast in the Lord: the humble shall hear thereof and be glad." Certainly, because the humble, being poor in spirit, know that if there is to be any amazing worth in themselves it is to come from God. Therefore, when they hear one as weak as themselves boasting in the Lord, they take heart. They rejoice with a glad hopefulness and expectancy.

Gratitude Out of Experience

What, then, is the secret of the gratitude of this singer? First, his gratitude is born of his own personal experience. He claims that he has been a seeker after God. "I sought the Lord," he tells us, with beautiful candor. He has been an explorer, an investigator in the realm of the spiritual. What has he found? He ought to be especially fitted to speak to this age that is so scientifically minded. We are concerned with facts; so is this seeker after God. Having sought, he reports his findings. I think we may listen to him with confidence. We may listen with the conviction that discoveries in the realm of the spiritual are no less valid than discoveries in the realm of the material. Having tested by experience, he has a right to speak. And mark you, it is only such who can speak with authority. This is true in every field of knowledge.

Suppose, now that Commander Byrd has returned to the United States, he should make statements about the south pole and its environs that I should feel disposed to dispute. Who would take me seriously? Men would say: "This brave explorer has ventured his life to see and to map the country of which he speaks. He has been there, while this preacher has never been beyond the equator." Therefore, I should be utterly discredited, and rightly so. But when some atheistic scientist or philosopher undertakes to speak on matters of religion, we often take him seriously, even though he has confessedly never been earnest enough to test by experience that of which he speaks. The wisest scholar in the world who has lived his life in willful ignorance of God has no more right to a hearing on the validity of our faith than has a mole on the reality and beauty of the sunrise.

Delivery from Fear

"I sought the Lord," says this sunny psalmist. Then what came of it? This is his confident answer: "He heard me and delivered me from all my fears." What a declaration! He had his fears. That is no doubt the reason he began to seek. We too seldom seek with seriousness till we get desperate. He was beset by tormenting terrors. He does not tell us that of which he was afraid. He may have been afraid of the loss of his wealth or of his health or of one dearly loved. He may have been afraid of the sins of his youth. He

may have been afraid of some foul habit that had taken
him captive and bound him hand and foot. He may
have been afraid of death or of that which might lie
beyond death. But whatever his fears, they were making his blood run cold as they closed about him like
wolves about a belated traveler at eventide. Besides,
he seemed utterly alone. As far as the eye could see
there was no promise of help. But, at last, in sheer
desperation he flung an empty, seeking hand out into
the gloom, and, lo, that hand was gripped and held
fast. He realized that he was no longer alone, but
that a Friend was at his side, a Friend whose presence
made these ghastly foes to vanish and brought in their
place a sweet sense of security and peace. And joyous
of heart and radiant of face he gave this testimony,
"He delivered me from all my fears."

And, second, this psalmist was grateful for what
God had done for others as well as for himself. For
instance, he had a friend with whom he was accustomed to share his spiritual experiences. That friend
had been overwhelmed by a veritable avalanche of
trouble. One disaster after another had come upon the
poor fellow till it seemed that he had been cheated of
all that makes life worth living. In fact, he was so
beaten down and trodden under foot by this besieging
army of troubles that he was no longer able to pray.
He could not put his agony into words. He could not
voice the tragic needs of his perplexed soul. What did
he do in this desperate plight? He cried, cried unto

the Lord, and the outcome of that pathetic cry was this, "The Lord heard him, and saved him out of all his troubles."

But this singer had other friends whose faces had for some reason lost their radiance and had come to wear the ugly mantle of a settled gloom. There were some, probably, whose faces were darkened by constant worry and care. There were some with peevish and fretful faces. There were envious faces and faces black with the hell of hate. There were sensual faces over which the cloven-footed demons of impurity had walked, leaving their ugly tracks at every step. There were sad faces, faces darkened by sorrow and wet with tears. But to all these a marvelous change had come; the gloom and the night had passed and a glorious dawn had transfigured them. So with gratitude he sings, "They looked unto him and became radiant."

Learning of God Most Important

Then this psalmist is grateful for what these experiences have taught him of God. He has learned of God at first hand; he has learned also from other saints. They have shared experiences. That is always helpful. The loss of the testimony meeting is no mean loss. It is ever a benediction for those who fear the Lord to speak one with another. Out of this sharing of experiences, above all, out of his own personal dealing with God, there had come to this ancient saint certain first-hand knowledge of God that filled his soul with grateful gladness. He knew God through experience. This is the crying need of our own day and of every day.

As a country school-teacher, far in the backwoods, I boarded in the home of a woman who was one of the choicest saints that it has ever been my privilege to know. I had known her in the years when she was a most commonplace, halting church member. I knew her also after she had passed through a wonderful religious experience. Every morning, when the duties of her housekeeping had been finished, she would take her Bible and retire into a little room that was all her own. Sometimes she would be gone only a very few minutes, sometimes for more than an hour. But when she came forth there always looked out from her eyes "the peace of a great discovery." My own faith, which was none too strong, was greatly strengthened by the fact that she "looked unto him and was radiant." That radiance has been an abiding benediction through the years.

II

Now what had this psalmist learned? Of what was he sure? Speaking out of his own heart-knowledge of God, he could say this: God is good.

To many to-day it seems trite to say that God is good, yet no discovery could be more gladsome. Nor could any be more revolutionary when we consider the spiritual darkness that abounded when this discovery was made. Think of the gods, cruel and lustful, of

the surrounding nations. Think of the false concep-
tions of God that were prevalent in Israel. Think of
your own conception of God. There are many experiences through which we pass even now, after Jesus
has come to reveal God, that make belief in the goodness of God exceedingly difficult. But this man, in
spite of his environment, in spite of the fact that he
had known suffering and heartache, was absolutely sure
that God is good.

He had discovered, too, that God is near. That, too,
is a marvelous discovery. How distant we often feel
he is as we stagger under our burden of weariness and
loneliness! But this man had come to realize that God
is always near, that he is constantly round about us,
that he is forever within the hearing of our voices and
within reach of our groping hands. This is true
amidst all circumstances of our lives. It is especially
true when the skies grow gray and the road stony.
Listen how tenderly he puts it, "The Lord is near unto
them that are of a broken heart."

God Is Sufficient

Finally, the psalmist has discovered that God is
always adequate. "I have constantly found him sufficient," he says joyously. He has never failed me; he
has never once let me down. When all other sources of
help have failed, I have found him abundantly adequate
for every need." As he sings his song, he can hear the
lions down the mountain side as they growl and snarl

in search of their prey.   In spite of the fact that they
are king of beasts, they are hungry.   They are in want.
Then with fine audacity he sets their snarls to music
as he sings, "The young lions do lack and suffer hunger,
but they that seek the Lord shall not want any good."

If David is the author of this Psalm, he wrote it
when he was a young man.   He had not then had the
vast experience of life that came to him through the
years.   But what did he have to say when youth had
gone and when songful summer had changed into
bleak winter?   This was a song of the Maytime.
What did he say amid the chills of December?   He
sang even more thrillingly of the sufficiency of God:
"The Lord is my Shepherd; I shall not want."   And
this is the verdict of all the saints.   "When I sent you
forth without purse and without scrip," Jesus asked
of his disciples, "lacked ye anything?"   And they
answered, "Nothing."   "He is always like that," says
this psalmist.   "He is always like that," declare those
through all the centuries who have really put him to
the test.   They have reached this common conclusion:
"My God shall supply every need of yours according
to his riches in glory by Christ Jesus."

III

"Now that is all well enough for this ancient saint,"
one says half angrily, "but he knew nothing of my situation.   He did not live in this bewildering age when
one support after another that we counted as secure has

been knocked from under us. Assuming that he found all this in God, of what value is it to me? Certainly I would give the world for such a gloriously radiant faith, but how may I find it? Who can put me on the road that leads to this desired goal? And this psalmist believes that he is equal to this high task. He is confident that there is a road to certainty, that what he has found all may find. And this is his direction: "Taste and see. Give God a chance, and you, too, will know that he is good, that he is ever near, that he is always sufficient."

Our Lord is abidingly eager to submit himself to the test of experience. Does he really hear prayer? There is only one way to be sure of it. Try him. Is he able to give strength in temptation? Try him. Can he really give victory over sin? Try him. Does he really comfort in sorrow? Try him. Does he indeed make all things new? Taste and see. Those who have tried him have found him sufficient. When Dr. J. H. Jowett was on his death bed, he wrote to a fellow minister who also was suffering. He wrote out of a rich personal experience. He had in some measure tested the sufficiency of Jesus for hours of stress and strain and difficulty. Among other things he wrote this fine, bracing word: "We have preached a great gospel, but remember that Jesus Christ is greater than anything we have ever said about him." This princely preacher has spoken grandly of Jesus, but he found that the half had

not, and could not, be put into words. There is only
one way to know, and that is by experience. So I close
with this appeal from this ancient saint, "O taste and
see that the Lord is good: blessed is the man that trust-
eth in him."

XVII

THE RECOVERED RAPTURE

Psalm 85: 6

"Wilt thou not revive us again: that thy people may rejoice in thee?"

I

My text is a prayer. It comes out of one of the most beautifully spiritual Psalms of the Bible. Here a patriot and saint is presenting before God a petition that he believes to be of vital importance both to himself and to his people. Devout souls through all the centuries have caught the cadences of his voice and have appreciated the worthfulness of his request. Having done so, they have been constrained to say "amen." As they have listened to his prayer they have been convinced that he was voicing the deepest hungers as well as the deepest needs of their hearts, and they have eagerly and earnestly made his petition their own. And I am wondering how many of us, as we hear his prayer, will feel constrained to mingle our voices with his. Frankly, I am afraid that the number will be none too great; for the petition that this saint is presenting is not vastly popular. There are multitudes to-day, even in the Church, who no longer say "amen" to this prayer. They rather remain utterly listless, or cry out

in protest, "Forbid it, Lord!"   For this psalmist is
praying for a revival.   Here is the petition that he is
bringing before God: "Revive us again: that thy people
may rejoice in thee."

There is nothing more evident than that the revival
has fallen upon evil days.   What announcement could
the average pastor make to his people next Sunday that
would create less enthusiasm, less approval, less holy
expectancy, than that he was soon to begin a revival?
Such an announcement would not guarantee the coming
together of an eager and enthusiastic congregation.   It
would have the very opposite effect.   There are many
churches in which the announcement of a revival would
have about as much drawing power as a notice that a
public collection was to be taken, or that the germs of
some contagious disease were to be put on exhibition.
For them, to be forewarned would be to be forearmed.
Many of the best people would be conspicuous by their
absence.   There would not be a rush to the church, but
rather an exodus from it.   It would be, "To your tents,
O Israel."

Yet it has not always been so.   The word revival was
once a winsome, thrilling word.   It was radiant with
life and beauty.   But such is not the case any more.
This summer I met for the first time in more than a
quarter of a century a girl with whom I had gone to our
village school when I was a lad.   I remembered her as
a vigorous, vivacious girl of unusual beauty.   But how
hardly the passing years had dealt with her.   They had

erased every vestige of her youthful charms. The cruel fists of suffering and sickness had so pounded her once lovely face and figure that it was impossible to see in that charred and tarnished bit of womanhood the slightest resemblance to the girl I had known in the springtime of life. So it is with this word revival. It has lost its charm. "It hath no form nor comeliness; and when we see it, there is no beauty that we should desire it."

II

Why is this the case? It is not because the idea of revival has fallen into disrepute in every department of life. It is only true in the realm of religion. For instance, nobody objects to a revival in nature. We all thrill at the coming of spring. This is especially true of those who live in our more northerly latitudes. How delightful when the first violet appears! How thrilling when the buds begin to swell; when the winter-stripped trees begin to deck themselves in their soft, verdant garments; when the catbird begins to sing among the apple blossoms; when the robin comes back from his sojourn in the far southland! When the spring comes we do not protest against its coming because it does not last all the year. We do not reject it because it is a climactic experience that will not abide. We are glad to welcome it in spite of this, because it means the coming of new life.

We do not object to revivals in these physical bodies of ours. Were you ever desperately ill, so ill that even to whisper was like lifting a heavy load, so ill that the most dainty dish only nauseated, so ill that life lost its tang and became little more than a wearisome burden? And then did you experience the joy of returning health, the passing of the pain, the coming of new strength, the return of the zest for living? Did you ever witness and rejoice over such a revival in one that you loved? I was in an automobile accident some years ago in which one very dear to me was rendered unconscious. She looked as if she were utterly dead. How welcome was the first quiver of an eyelash! How welcome the first incoherent word that showed that a revival was on and that life was coming back!

Do you know the most welcome message that I could possibly bring to you this morning? Suppose I could tell you with authority that a revival in business was on the way, that it was just over the rim of the horizon and would be upon us to-morrow. Suppose I could say to you with certainty, "To-morrow your assets will double in value; to-morrow you will get your lost position back; to-morrow your decrease in salary will become an increase." What enthusiasm that would create! It would be flashed from city to city and from continent to continent till almost every nation and tribe would hear the news before nightfall. But when we begin to speak of a revival in religion our interest wanes, our minds wander, we slip into a comatose state and wonder how soon the tiresome ordeal will be over.

Why are many so indifferent to a revival of religion?

Why are many even antagonistic? There are a number of reasons. I am going to mention two.

1. The revival has been rendered unattractive and even odious to some because they have seen only its counterfeit. They do not distinguish the real from the spurious. We confess at once that there have been many so-called revivals that have not really revived. It is not my purpose to say who is most to blame for this. There are those who put the whole weight of responsibility upon the professional evangelist. Part of the blame surely belongs there, but not the whole of it. There is a type of professional evangelist whose ministry, I fear, has been nothing short of a menace to the Church. But there is surely another type whose ministry has been enriching. We cannot, therefore, shift the whole blame upon his shoulders. Part of it rests on us who are pastors, part of it upon our congregations. Too often all of us have undertaken to enter into this spiritual enrichment by some other way rather than by the door. We have demanded the harvest without the necessary cultivation. Therefore there have been many so-called revivals that have brought death rather than life.

But it is neither fair nor reasonable to discredit a reality because that reality is sometimes counterfeited. By revival, mark you, I am not speaking of any particular form of revival, ancient or modern. No more am I speaking of any certain method. By revival I mean a spiritual awakening. A revival takes place when the heart recaptures its first rapture; when the soul recovers its first love. That the revival in some form has been mightily used for the bringing in of the kingdom of God in the past, no student of Church history can deny. I am unwilling, therefore, to throw the revival away simply because it has been counterfeited. In fact, I am convinced that such climactic experiences are necessary for the highest spiritual attainment, both of the individual and of the Church. You are not going to toss aside the diamond that you wear because there are jewels very much like it that are made of paste. I am not going to throw away what little money I have in my pocket because there is such worthless stuff in the world as counterfeit money. Let us remember that no amount of sham can destroy what is real.

2. My second reason for our widespread indifference and antagonism to the revival is just this: The modern Church is to a great extent an ease-loving Church. Such being the case, too often it is not willing to pay the price that a revival costs. At times we hate our deadness, our lack of spiritual beauty, but we hate still more to be bothered. That may sound a bit pessimistic and unkind, I know, but I am confident that the facts in the case bear witness to its truth. There are many, doubtless, who would like to have a revival, provided it could be had without any serious trouble. But such is not the case. A revival is costly. It always has been. It always will be. Some months ago a gentle-

man drove a beautiful sport model Cadillac up in front of my home and came in and said to me with great enthusiasm: "There is the car you ought to have. You are in the Cadillac class." That was really a word fitly spoken. I had never thought of it after that fashion before. He told me, also, what an honor it would be to have one in my position driving a Cadillac about the city. His final word was that it cost only so many thousand dollars, a mere pittance for one in my position. That quenched all my enthusiasm. I even forgot the warm glow that was created by being reminded that I belonged in the Cadillac class. I said to him frankly: "Thank you, but I do not want your car." Now when I said that I did not mean that his car was undesirable. I did not mean that I would not trade with him under any circumstances. Had he set the price at four thousand cents instead of four thousand dollars, had he promised further to endow the car, possibly we could have traded. But when the price and upkeep were taken into consideration, I had to say frankly and honestly: "I do not desire your car." Such is the case with a revival. Even where we desire one, we do not always desire it genuinely enough to pay the price.

Hosea gives us some idea of the price to be paid as he pleads for a revival in his day. "Break up your fallow ground," he cries with passionate earnestness. "Break up your fallow ground: for it is time to seek the Lord, till he come and rain righteousness upon you." That word takes us out on the farm. Spring-time has come and we are getting ready for the planting and the sowing. But how do we go about it? We do not plant the seed among the weeds and briers and sprouts that have grown up during the year. True, the ground is fallow. That is, it is not new ground that has never been furrowed by a plow. It is ground that has been under cultivation; but in spite of that, it needs to be plowed again. The farmer only wastes his seed who sows them in unprepared soil. So our hearts that have been broken must be broken anew, broken by repentance, before there can be a revival. God is always eager to give, but he cannot give what we refuse to take. He cannot thrust life into hands that are too full of things to receive it. The revival always begins, not by the gathering in of those without the Church, but with the deeper consecration of those within. The Church, therefore, that would experience a revival must repent.

And by repentance we mean something more than the giving up of our positive wrongdoing. Of course this is included. We surely need to repent of our forgotten vows, our uncharitable judgments, our open transgressions of God's law. But we need even more, if possible, to repent of failure to adequately represent our Lord. We need to repent of our lack of prayer and of our resulting lack of power. We need to repent of the shameful way we have shunted God's cause into second, third, or hundredth place, instead of putting first things first. We need to repent of our listlessness, our cruel indifference, as we have faced the desperate plight of men in need. We need to repent of our spiritual barrenness. "When Zion travaileth she brings forth children." But just as there are parents that are too selfish to desire children, even so there are churches that are too selfish to desire spiritual children. There are hundreds of churches in our own communion, who, last year, did not report one single addition on profession of faith. Surely this is proof positive that we need to repent with that true repentance that means, not simply to be sorry, but to be so sorry that we shall face about and courageously share with our Lord the burden of a world gone wrong.

What, then, is the meaning of the cry that we hear on every hand to-day, "The revival is a thing of the past"? Some are saying it gleefully, some listlessly, some wistfully. But if this is true, why is it true? It is certainly not because human nature has changed. The heart of humanity remains the same through all the years. It is not because the Divine Nature has changed. Jesus Christ is the same yesterday, to-day, and forever. It is not because revivals are no longer possible. Let any pastor to-day unite with any group, large or small, in any church, in any city, village, or countryside; and let these say from their hearts, "Give me or I die," and what will be the result? Then and there a spiritual awakening will take place as surely as night follows day. To speak more accurately, a revival has already begun. But such an adventure is rather too exacting for our timid souls. It is easier to talk the commodity down than to pay the price necessary to our possession of it. It is easier to school ourselves to regard it as of little worth than to claim it as our own.

> "Upon a rock stands prone my soul,
>   A diver, lean, undressed,
> And looks and fears the shock, and turns,
>   And hides his shame in some poor, sorry jest."

III

But the fact that so many, both within and without our churches, do not desire a revival to-day is by no means proof positive that a revival is not needed. It is rather an indication of the greater need. One said recently with a glint of humor in his eye, "It is as hard to-day to convict man of sin as it is to convict a bootlegger in the courts of New York for selling liquor." But this does not prove in the least that either the sinner or the bootlegger is blameless. When Samson waked from his guilty sleep and went out to meet the enemy that he had triumphed over again and again, he was conscious of no great change in himself. Had you told him that his strength had departed, that his inner light had failed, that God was no longer with him, he would doubtless have given you a hot denial. But the fact that he did not realize his loss did not in any sense prevent that loss from being a reality. The fact that he was unconscious of his danger did not lessen or destroy his danger; it rather increased it. His lack of any sense of need made his blindness, his shackles, and his slavery inevitable.

We read of a certain church that passed a resolution with regard to itself that read somewhat after this fashion: Whereas we have the best pastor in the city, and whereas we have the best choir and choir leader, and whereas we have the most select congregation, be it resolved that we are rich and increased in goods and have need of nothing. But the fact that they thought themselves rich did not make them rich in reality. As Jesus saw them as they really were, he had to declare broken-heartedly that, in spite of their boasted wealth, they were in reality "wretched and miserable and poor and blind and naked."

A few days ago a friend of mine was attending a baseball game. When he was ready to go home his right limb seemed to be asleep, and he walked away with a limp. When he reached home the sense of sleepiness and deadness increased rather than diminished. At last he noticed that his limb had lost all sensitiveness. A pin prick did not cause him the least pain. What did he do? He did not call in his friends to rejoice with him that he had lost his sensitiveness. He rather called in a physician. He knew that such loss did not denote health, but sickness; not life, but partial death. And our present loss of spiritual sensitiveness, our lack of that passionate hunger for righteousness that amounts to positive pain, these are not an indication of vigorous spiritual health.   They rather indicate the opposite.

But I am sure that even those who do not believe that we need a revival will agree to this: We are desperately in need of something.   No one who is not spiritually blind can be satisfied with present conditions. There is no shutting our eyes to the fact that there is abroad a dreadful decay of idealism, that moral standards that have been the underpinnings of our whole social order are being lightly thrown away.   The atmosphere in which we move is, as a rule, not spiritually invigorating.   It is rather enervating.   It tends, to an unusual degree, to weaken our moral fiber.   So much is this the case that, again and again, we see men upon whose integrity we would have staked our very lives, proving utterly unworthy of the confidence that their fellows have reposed in them.   In great measure we have cast off restraint.   There is a veritable orgy of doing as we please.   The biggest business in our nation is the crime business.   Our plight may be most nearly described by that tragic sentence in Judges: "Every man did that which was right in his own eyes."   Surely, then, if we do not need a revival, we are in desperate need of something that can meet our needs.

IV

What is that something that we need?   Bearing in mind that we mean by a revival not a certain form, but a rediscovery of God, it is my firm conviction that the supreme need of this hour is for a revival of religion. This conviction, in spite of widespread indifference, and even antagonism, I am sure I share with many others. We believe in the revival because we believe in God. We are convinced that the revival is an absolute necessity because we believe that God is an absolute necessity. When Ezekiel went into the valley of dry bones, it never occurred to him that he could raise up "an exceeding great army" by merely polishing and organizing those bones. He knew that the breath of God must breathe upon those slain before there could be any life. "Where there is no vision," said a wise man long ago, "the people cast off restraint." The one hope then for the cure of this deadly evil is the recovery of our vision of God. Legislation is not enough. Even the preaching of a high standard of ethics is not enough. There was never more ethical preaching than to-day. We hear it on every hand. But somehow these ethics are not always put into practice. We have glimpsed the bag of gold at the end of the rainbow, but the goddess of the mist flees at our approach, taking her treasure with her. Our psalmist realized this futility of the doctoring of the outside of life. Therefore he prayed, "Revive us again: that thy people may rejoice in thee."

A real revival means a rebirth of joy, and that is a commodity on which the modern Church is exceedingly short. But this joy is something far greater than a mere tide of emotion. It is a joy that is the natural outcome of abounding spiritual life.   It is a joy that means the changing of our want into wealth, our timidity into courage, our weakness into strength, our pathetic pessimism into glowing hope.   It means the rekindling of our burnt-out enthusiasms and the re-birth of a fiery earnestness.   It means a new passion for the saving of men and for the spreading of the kingdom of God to the uttermost parts of the earth. It tends to the making of the Church a truly glorious Church without spot or wrinkle or any such thing. And enriching the Church it enriches the world.   "God be merciful to us, and bless us; and cause thy face to shine upon us."   That is good, but it does not end there. The final outcome is this : "That thy way may be known upon earth, thy saving health among all nations."   This is a sick world, but there is a remedy.   There is a balm to make the wounded whole.   Because we believe this, let us pray together now, and till he comes and rains righteousness upon us, this great prayer : "Revive us again : that thy people may rejoice in thee."